Video

D0717299

Questions and Answers books are available on the following subjects:

Amateur Radio
Automobile Steering & Suspension
Automobile Brakes & Braking
Automobile Electrical Systems
Automobile Engines
Automobile Transmission Systems
BASIC Programming
Brickwork & Blockwork
Cameras
Car Body Care & Repair
Carpentry & Joinery
CB Radio
Central Heating
Colour Television
Cycles & Cycling
Diesel Engines
Domestic Lighting
Electric Arc Welding
Electric Motors
Electric Wiring
Electricity
Electronics
Gas Shielded Arc Welding
Gas Welding & Cutting

Gems
GRP Boat Construction
Hi-Fi
Home Insulation
Household Security
Integrated Circuits
Lathework
Light Commercial Vehicles
Microprocessors
Motorcycles
Painting & Decorating
Personal Computing
Pipework & Pipewelding
Plastering
Plumbing
Radio & Television
Radio Repair
Refrigeration
Steel Boat Construction
Transistors
Video
Videocassette Recorders
Wooden Boat Construction
Yacht & Boat Design

QUESTIONS & ANSWERS

Video

Steve Money

Newnes Technical Books

Newnes Technical Books

is an imprint of the Butterworth Group
which has principal offices in
London, Boston, Durban, Singapore, Sydney, Toronto, Wellington

First published 1981
Second edition 1983

© Butterworth & Co. (Publishers) Ltd, 1983

British Library Cataloguing in Publication Data

Money, S. A.
  Video – 2nd ed. – (Questions and answers)
  1. Video tape recorders and recording
  I. Title   II. Series
  621.388   TK6655.V5

  ISBN 0-408-01384-2

Library of Congress Cataloguing in Publication Data

Money, Steve A.
  Video.
  (Questions and answers)
  Includes index.
  Home video systems. I. Title. II. Series.
TK9960.M58 1983 621.388'33 83-12175
ISBN 0-408-01384-2

Photoset by Butterworths Litho Preparation Department
Printed in England by Whistable Litho Ltd, Whitstable, Kent

Contents

Preface

In recent years an important development in home entertainment has been the arrival of the home video recorder. These machines can readily be used to record broadcast television programmes and to play back pre-recorded tapes. Many users of home video recorders have also obtained video cameras so that they can produce the video equivalent of home movies. Portable recorders and single-unit camera-recorders make it possible for the user to operate outdoors, and it seems likely that video will gradually replace home movies using 8 mm film.

Television itself has seen the arrival of colour, information services such as teletext and viewdata, and more recently broadcasting via space satellites. Video discs, video games and home computers have also taken their place in the home entertainment scene.

This book explains in simple terms the basic technical aspects of these developments in television and video technology. Since all are based upon television principles or make use of a television display, the early chapters review the principles of television, video displays and colour television techniques; this includes a brief introduction to television broadcasting and reception via space satellites. Later chapters cover the principles of video recording, including the characteristics of the three popular home video formats (VHS, Beta and V2000) and of portable video recorders and camcorders. A chapter has been devoted to the principles of operation of video cameras, particularly home video colour cameras. Finally there are sections dealing with videotex systems such as teletext and viewdata, the major video disc formats, and the principles of video games systems.

S.M.

1
Principles of video

What is video?

The term 'video' is roughly synonymous with television (TV). It was originally used to mean the signals and circuits which dealt with picture information in a television system, but while television refers specifically to the broadcasting of picture signals using radio waves, video today covers the broader uses of television techniques, such as surveillance in security systems, industrial monitoring, and recording of signals.

Video signals from a camera or TV broadcast can now be recorded on magnetic tape in much the same way as audio signals are, although different techniques are used. This gives the electronic equivalent of a home movie using cine film. Video discs are also available which, like gramophone discs, allow playback of recorded programmes, providing both sound and vision from the same disc.

Recently, text and graphic information systems, such as teletext and viewdata, have appeared. These can be considered as video systems since they use television for the display, and in teletext the signals themselves are sent out with the television picture signal.

Video games and some home computer systems also use the domestic TV set as a display and can be regarded as video equipment.

1

How does television work?

The basic scheme of a television system is shown in Fig. 1. At the transmitting end, a TV camera is used to convert the image of the

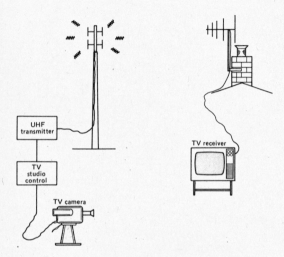

Fig. 1. *Basic scheme for television*

scene being televised into electrical signals. Inside the camera, the image is focussed on to a photoelectric device, which produces an electrical change proportional to the amount of light falling on it. In order to resolve the details of the scene, the image is scanned in a series of horizontal lines. As the scan moves along each line, the variations in brightness of points along it produce a varying signal from the photoelectric device. This video signal is used to modulate a VHF or UHF radio transmitter, which broadcasts the programme.

At the receiving end, the signals are picked up by an aerial, amplified, and then used to produce a display on a cathode ray tube. Here the screen is scanned in the same way as at the transmitter, and the video signal is used to vary the brightness of points on the scan-lines to build up a reproduction of the image being televised. It is important for the sending and receiving scans to be synchronised, so additional signals are transmitted for this purpose. Other parts of the broadcast signal convey the sound for the programme, and colour information.

In closed-circuit systems for industrial monitoring or educational uses, cable transmission is used instead of radio.

How are moving pictures produced on television?

Both cine film and television make use of the phenomenon of persistence of vision to create the illusion of moving pictures. The retina of the human eye does not respond instantaneously to changes in light but retains each image for about a fifteenth of a second. If a sequence of slightly different images is presented to the eye in rapid succession, the retina merges the individual images together to give what appears to be a moving picture.

In the cinema, pictures ('frames') are presented at a rate of 24 per second. In most television systems, the picture rate is set at 25 per second, which can conveniently be synchronised to the mains power supply frequency of 50 Hz. In America and Japan, where the supply frequency is 60 Hz, the television picture rate is set at 30 pictures per second.

How many scan-lines are used?

The first regular television broadcast service, which started in Britain in 1936, used 405 scan-lines and 25 frames per second, with interlaced scanning. This system still operates today as a secondary service.

Scanning systems with 441 lines and 819 lines were used for many years in France but have now been discontinued. Most countries in the world have now adopted the 625 line standard with interlaced scanning, but America and Japan use a scanning standard of 525 lines.

3

What is interlaced scanning and why is it used?

One problem which arises in both cinema films and television is flicker. Although the eye is unable to distinguish individual pictures when shown at 25 per second, it can sense flickering light as they flash on the screen. This flickering effect can be very annoying, but it disappears if the picture rate is increased to about 50 per second. (We are not aware of the flicker from an electric light bulb running on a 50 Hz mains supply.) In the cinema, a multibladed shutter is used in the projector so that each frame of the film is flashed on to the screen twice, giving a flicker rate of 48 per second, and a similar technique is employed in television.

In television, the picture rate could simply be raised to 50 per second, but this would increase the bandwidth of the video signal by a factor of two and is undesirable. An alternative method, and the one normally used, is interlaced scanning. The picture is scanned at 50 times a second for the required flicker rate, but only half the lines are traced out on each scan. On the first scan, the lines are spread out so that there is a one-line gap between adjacent lines. On the second scan, the remaining lines are used to fill in the gaps in the first scan. Each scan is called a 'field' and is labelled odd or even. In effect, the two field scans interlace with one another as in Fig. 2. This is achieved by making the total lines

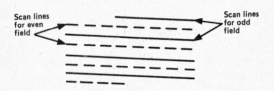

Fig. 2. Principle of interlaced scanning

in a complete frame or picture an odd number so that each field contains an odd half-line. When traced out on the screen, one field will be displaced half a line relative to the other so that its scan lines fall in the gaps between the scan lines of the other field.

With interlaced scanning, the flicker rate is doubled, but since the information being transmitted is the same, the bandwidth is unaffected.

How is picture synchronisation achieved?

In any television system, if the received picture is to be properly reconstructed, the scan systems at transmitter and receiver must be properly synchronised. This is achieved by adding a series of synchronising pulses to the video signal.

At the start of each scan-line, there is a line sync pulse to ensure that the transmitter and receiver scans are started at the same time. Similarly, at the start of each of the field scans, further pulses are added to synchronise the start of the field scan. The field sync pulses are broken into half-line segments to maintain line sync and to help in achieving correct interlacing of the scans. Other pulses, known as 'equalising pulses', are also included to reduce the disturbance in signal level caused by the wide field sync pulses.

To enable the synchronisation pulse signals to be separated easily from the picture information, they are set below the black level of the video signal, as shown in Fig. 3. The sync pulse is normally 30 per cent of the complete video signal for peak white.

Following the field sync pulses, there are usually some 20 black scan-lines where the video signal is held at the black level. These blank lines form a black margin at the top and bottom of the screen and allow the scan circuits at both transmitter and receiver to carry out the retrace from the bottom right-hand corner to the top left-hand of the screen ready for the next field scan.

Before and after each line sync pulse, the signal is held at black level for a short time to produce what are known as the front and back 'porches'. This is done to allow the video amplifier circuits to settle after the sync pulse and before the picture signal proper starts. The effect on the screen is to produce a black margin at each side, but in most receivers the scan is increased to place this outside the screen area.

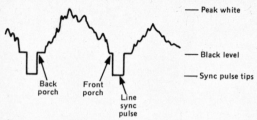

Fig. 3(a). Video signal around line sync pulse, showing front and back porches

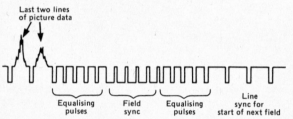

Fig. 3(b). Field sync pulse pattern, showing the equalising pulses

What is the video signal bandwidth?

At the low-frequency end, the video signal extends to d.c., since any change in the d.c. level of the signal will correspond to a change in average brightness of the display on the screen.

The high-frequency end of the video signal band will be determined by the degree of horizontal resolution required in the picture. For a 625-line system, only some 575 are used for the picture, since the others are blanked during field retrace periods. Suppose we allow a similar resolution in the horizontal direction, so that each scan line would contain 575 picture elements. The highest frequency will occur when the elements along the line are alternately black and white. This produces a square wave, where each cycle consists of a pair of adjacent picture elements.

For 625-line systems, one complete line scan has a duration of 64 microseconds. Subtracting the time used for a sync pulse plus front and back porches, the picture signal occupies 51 microseconds, and within this time there will be 288 cycles of video waveform. This gives a maximum frequency of some 5.5 MHz for the video signal. The British 625-line system has a video bandwidth of 5.5 MHz, but countries with 625-line systems normally use a bandwidth of only 5 MHz, giving slightly less resolution. The American 525-line system has a bandwidth of 4.2 MHz.

What happens to the television sound signal?

In the old British 405-line system, sound was amplitude-modulated on to a carrier signal 3.5 MHz lower in frequency than the vision carrier. For 525- and 625-line systems, frequency modulation is normally used for the sound signal. The carrier frequency is varied in sympathy with the amplitude variations of the audio signal in the same way as for VHF radio broadcasting.

For the British 625-line transmissions, the sound uses a sub-carrier of 6 MHz which is then added to the vision part of the signal for modulation on to the UHF carrier frequency. Other 625-line systems use a 5.5 MHz sound subcarrier, while the American 525-line system has a 4.5 MHz sound subcarrier.

What is vestigial sideband transmission?

When a carrier signal is amplitude modulated by a video signal, a range of new signals is produced on each side of the original carrier frequency. These signals, called 'sidebands', represent the sum and difference components of the carrier and video frequencies. The result is a band of signals as shown in Fig. 4a.

The two sidebands contain identical information, and in the receiver only one is needed to recover the video signal. In order to conserve space in the available frequency bands, only one sideband is transmitted, the other sideband being filtered out before the signal reaches the aerial. In practice, part of the unwanted sideband does go through the filter to leave a signal transmission band, as shown in Fig. 4b. This mode of transmission is called 'vestigial sideband' for obvious reasons.

7

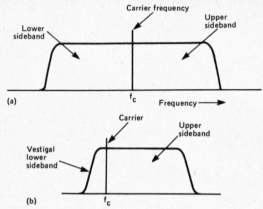

Fig. 4. (a) Normal amplitude modulation showing two sidebands.
(b) Vestigial sideband transmission with lower sideband filtered out

How does satellite TV broadcasting work?

For some years now television signals have been relayed via space
satellites for the transfer of news items and programmes between
the world's broadcasting networks. Some satellites are used to
distribute programmes to cable networks, and recently direct
broadcasting satellites (DBS) have been set up to transmit programmes directly to individual viewers.

The satellites are placed in a 'geostationary' orbit 22 000 miles
above the earth so that they remain over a fixed point on the
equator and are therefore at a fixed point in the sky relative to the
ground stations. This avoids the need for steerable aerials to track
the satellites.

Each satellite carries several 'transponders', each consisting of a
receiver to pick up signals from a ground station and a transmitter to send signals down to other ground stations. Relay satellites
use an 'uplink' frequency of around 6 GHz (6000 MHz) and a
'downlink' in the 4 GHz band. For broadcasting an uplink of
14 GHz or 17 GHz is used, and the signals are broadcast back to

earth on about 12 GHz. Each transponder carries several television channels as well as thousands of telephone and data communications channels.

What frequency bands are used for television broadcasting?

Because of the wide bandwidth of the combined sound and vision signal, all television broadcasting is carried out in the very high frequency (VHF), ultra high frequency (UHF) or microwave bands. The normal ground-based broadcast network uses what are known as bands I, II, IV and V, while satellite transmissions use the microwave bands. Band II is used for FM radio broadcasting. Frequencies and channels used are:

Band I (VHF)	41–80 MHz	Channels 1 to 5
Band III (VHF)	175–220 MHz	Channels 6 to 14
Band IV/V (UHF)	470–860 MHz	Channels 21 to 69
Satellite	11.76–12.5 GHz	Channels 1 to 40

In Britain bands I and III were used for the original 405-line TV service, which is being phased out. Future use of these bands is under discussion. European countries use bands I and III for main transmitters, but channel-numbering for these bands is slightly different from that used in Britain. All services use the 625-line system. In North America the band and channel numbering is similar, but a 525-line TV system is used.

Satellite TV channels are typically 20 MHz wide, and each satellite handles several channels.

In America satellites with 4–6 GHz transponders are used to relay programmes to cable TV and community TV systems. Typical of these services are Home Box Office and Cable News Network. Some home viewers also have installed dish aerials and receivers to pick up these transmissions, although they are not really intended as a public broadcasting service. The Russian Gorizont satellites are also used as TV relays to carry the Moscow service to remote parts of Russia, and these 4 GHz transmissions can be received quite well throughout Europe since the satellite itself is located over the Atlantic ocean.

9

2
Television reception

How is television received?

Modern television receivers invariably make use of the super-
heterodyne principle, in which the incoming VHF or UHF signals
from the aerial are changed into a fixed intermediate frequency
(IF) signal at which most of the amplification of the signal is
carried out. Fig. 5 shows the arrangement of a typical television
receiver system.

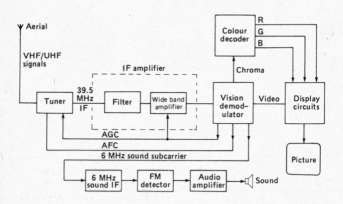

Fig. 5. *Basic TV receiver system*

Signals picked up by the aerial pass first to a tuner unit where, after some amplification, signals from the desired channel are converted to the intermediate frequency.

The IF amplifier section has a bandpass characteristic similar to that shown in Fig. 6. The response is fairly flat over a passband of

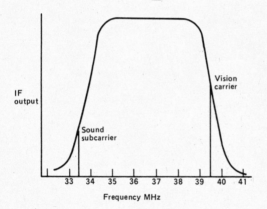

Fig. 6. *Typical IF amplifier frequency response*

some 4 to 5 MHz, to allow the wide-band vision signal through, but falls off rapidly above and below the passband so that any signals picked up from the adjacent television channels will be rejected. In Britain, the vision carrier is normally set at 39.5 MHz, while the sound subcarrier falls at 33.5 MHz. In continental Europe, the IF bandpass is slightly narrower but the frequencies used are similar. In the USA and Japan, frequencies of 41–45 MHz are used in the IF amplifier.

Older types of television receiver achieve the desired bandpass characteristic by using a number of tuned amplifier stages in cascade, but modern receivers generally use a block filter to give the desired bandpass, followed by a wideband untuned amplifier as shown in Fig. 5. This arrangement is more suitable when an integrated circuit IF amplifier is to be used. The filter section may consist of a number of normal tuned circuits coupled together and adjusted to produce the desired response or may use a surface acoustic wave (SAW) type of device.

After amplification, the IF signal is demodulated to give the actual video signal, and after further amplification this signal is used to drive the display circuits and produce the picture on the screen.

The sound signal appears at the output of the vision demodulator as a 6 MHz carrier signal, and this is separated out and amplified in the 6 MHz sound IF amplifier. Finally, the sound IF signal passes to an FM discriminator to extract the audio signal which eventually drives the loudspeaker. In order to avoid a buzz on sound and possible patterning on the picture, the sound subcarrier signal at 33.5 MHz is reduced to about 3 per cent of its normal level before it reaches the vision demodulator stage.

Apart from the signal and display circuits, a television receiver also contains several low and high voltage power supplies. Normally, the power for the receiver is obtained from the domestic mains supply, but some receivers can also be operated from either a 12 V car battery or internal rechargeable batteries, making them portable.

What is inside a TV tuner unit?

A typical television tuner unit is arranged as shown in Fig. 7.

After some amplification, the signal from the aerial is passed to a mixer stage. This usually consists of an amplifier which is biassed so that its characteristics are non-linear. In the mixer, the input signal is combined with another signal generated by a local oscillator in the tuner unit. Because of its non-linear operation, the mixer will produce at its output two new signals with frequencies equal to the sum and difference of the input and local oscillator frequencies. A tuned circuit at the output of the mixer is used to select the difference frequency and reject the other signals.

The local oscillator is offset from the desired input frequency by an amount equal to the intermediate frequency. Signals from the desired channel will produce at the mixer output a difference frequency equal to the intermediate frequency, while other channels will produce signals above and below the IF which will be rejected by the IF amplifier. Tuning the oscillator frequency will allow any desired channel to be converted to the intermediate frequency. The aerial and mixer input tuned circuits are also varied so that they track roughly with the oscillator tuning.

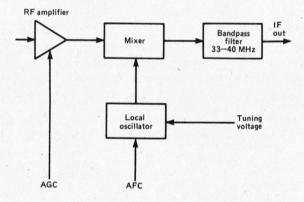

Fig. 7. Block diagram of typical TV tuner

Mixer stages generate more noise than simple amplifier stages, so in order to ensure good signal-to-noise ratio, it is usual to amplify the input signals by a factor of 10 or so before they are passed to the mixer. The amplifier stage also prevents the local oscillator signals from being coupled into the aerial circuit, from which they could be radiated and cause interference to neighbouring TV receivers.

In older designs of receiver, the tuning of the input, mixer, and local oscillator circuits is controlled by a set of variable capacitors ganged together on a common shaft. Station selection may be by means of a tuning dial or by a set of cams operated by

13

pushbuttons. Modern receivers use varactor diodes instead of the tuning capacitors, and tuning adjustment is by varying the voltage applied to the diodes. Channels are selected by using pushbuttons to set up one of a number of preset tuning voltages. In some sets, touch-sensitive switches replace the pushbuttons. Other receivers have remote control units allowing channels to be changed from the viewer's chair.

Some more advanced TV receivers use digital synthesiser systems to replace the local oscillator in the tuner. Here the actual station frequency or channel number may be keyed in from a small calculator-style keyboard. Such receivers may also have facilities for automatically scanning through the band to select each station in turn.

What is a varactor diode and how does it work?

A varactor diode is a silicon junction diode which acts as a variable capacitor whose value can be changed by varying the voltage applied across the diode. These devices are also called 'varicap' (variable capacitance) diodes.

Any junction diode will act as a variable capacitor when it is reverse biassed, but varactor diodes are specially designed to give a wide range of capacitance and to give low loss operation at high frequencies.

A typical junction diode consists of a block of silicon in which one part has been doped to make it n-type silicon and the remainder has been doped to produce p-type silicon. In n-type silicon, there are surplus electrons which migrate among the atoms of the material and can act as negative charge carriers. P-type, on the other hand, contains positive charge carriers which are referred to as 'holes'. In Fig. 8a, the charge carriers are shown as plus and minus signs.

When the anode (p-side) of a diode is biassed positive relative to the cathode (n-side), the electrons and holes are drawn across the junction by the applied voltage and a current flows through the diode. If the applied voltage is reversed, the electrons and holes are repelled away from the junction, leaving a very thin layer on each side of the junction which contains no charge carriers and therefore acts as an insulator. In these conditions, very little current can flow.

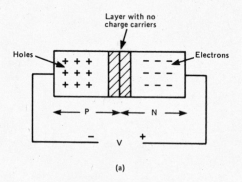

(a)

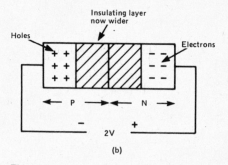

(b)

Fig. 8. (a) Low reverse bias on p-n diode produces narrow gap and high capacitance. *(b)* Increased reverse voltage gives wider gap and reduced capacitance

When the diode is reverse-biassed, it will effectively be a capacitor, since it consists of two plates separated by a thin insulator. If the reverse voltage is increased, the electrons and

15

holes move further from the junction, leaving a thicker insulating layer and reducing the value of the diode capacitance since the plates have been moved apart. This is shown in Fig. 8b.

A typical circuit for a varactor tuning control is shown in Fig. 9. Here a stabilised voltage is applied across a series of potentiometers, and the preset voltage from one of these is selected and

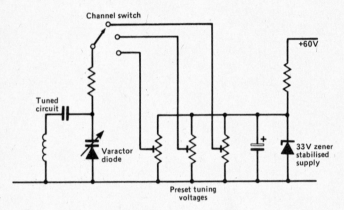

Fig. 9. Typical varactor diode tuning scheme

used to reverse bias the varactor diodes. Each potentiometer is preset to tune the tuner circuits to a different channel and may be selected by the pushbutton switch.

What is a frequency synthesiser and how does it work?

Fig. 10 shows a block diagram for a typical digital frequency synthesiser system.

A varactor tuned oscillator generates a signal with a frequency f_o which is passed through a digital frequency divider circuit having a division ratio n. The divider is in fact basically a digital counter type of circuit which produces at its output a frequency f_o/n.

16

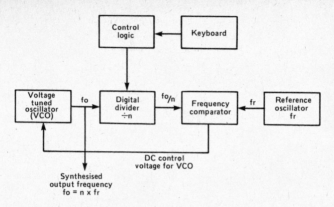

Fig. 10. *Basic block diagram of frequency synthesiser*

The output from the divider is fed to a discriminator circuit in which its frequency is compared with that of an accurate, quartz crystal controlled, reference oscillator of frequency f_r. A voltage proportional to the difference in frequency between f_o/n and f_r is produced and this is fed to the varactor to vary the frequency f_o. If there is sufficient gain in the feedback loop, the frequency f_o will now change until $f_o/n = f_r$, which means that $f_o = n \times f_r$.

Suppose f_r is 1 MHz and the division ratio n is set at 450, then the circuit will settle down with $f_o = 450$ MHz. Now by altering the division ratio, the frequency f_o can be set to any desired multiple of 1 MHz.

By using suitable digital logic, the ratio n and hence the frequency can be set up by merely keying in numbers from a calculator-style keyboard. A microprocessor can also be used to control the division ratio; here the channel number can be keyed in and the processor converts this to the proper frequency value and sets up the synthesiser. The receiver can also be made to scan through the frequency band by stepping the divider ratio until a station is found. The frequency of that station can now be stored in a digital memory. The scan can then be continued until the frequencies of all available stations have been stored away.

Stations can now be selected by merely recalling the contents of the appropriate digital memory and using them to set up the synthesiser. Some more sophisticated video cassette recorders use this method for setting up their tuner systems.

How does a touch switch work?

Modern TV receivers often use touch switches instead of push-button switches for channel selection. Fig. 11 shows the basic circuit for such a switch. The switch is operated by placing a

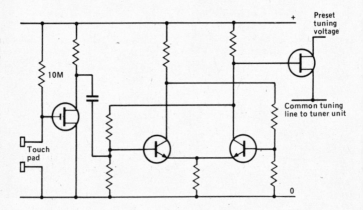

Fig. 11. *Typical touch switch circuit*

fingertip across two bare metal electrodes. One electrode is grounded or connected to a small negative voltage; the other is connected to a positive potential through a very high resistance and also feeds the gate electrode of a MOS field effect transistor. In normal conditions, there is a positive potential applied to the FET gate, since its input impedance is very high. The FET is therefore normally turned on. If a fingertip is used to bridge the contacts, it presents a relatively low resistance to ground and reduces the positive potential to the FET, causing it to turn off. The pulse at the drain electrode of the FET triggers a latch circuit which in turn switches on another FET to couple the preset voltage from a tuning potentiometer to the varactors in the tuner unit.

Normally, there will be one touch switch for each channel. They are interconnected so that when one latch is turned on, it automatically resets the other latches and only one tuning voltage is selected at a time. The latches may also be used to drive neon lamps or light-emitting diodes (LEDs) to indicate which switch has been selected. Most systems use an integrated circuit for the switch and latch circuits, with perhaps six or eight switches built into a single integrated circuit.

How does remote control work?

Remote control systems for television fall into two main groups according to the method by which control signals are transmitted from the hand-held unit to the receiver. One type uses ultrasonic waves; the other uses a beam of infrared light.

In the ultrasonic system, a piezoelectric transducer in the remote transmitter unit is driven by a signal with a frequency of about 40 kHz. Piezoelectric material has the property of converting the electrical signal into mechanical vibration which produces a high-frequency (40 kHz) sound wave. When the transmitter is aimed in the direction of the TV receiver, a second piezoelectric transducer in the TV set picks up the sound wave and converts it back into an electrical signal.

The infrared system uses an LED which emits a beam of infrared light when energised by an electrical signal. The beam of infrared light is detected at the TV receiver by a photocell which produces an electrical control signal.

Various techniques are used for conveying the control commands over the ultrasonic or infrared transmission link. In the simpler systems, a pulse transmitted from the remote unit is used to step a digital counter circuit in the TV set. This digital counter selects the available channels one at a time in sequence. With this scheme the remote-control button is pressed a number of times until the desired channel has been selected by the counter.

More sophisticated control systems use a pulse coding technique in which each command is represented by a unique sequence of pulses transmitted over the link. Fig. 12 shows the general idea

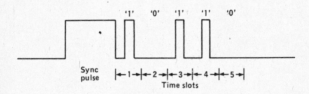

Fig. 12. Digital pulse coding for remote control

of such a pulse code. At the start of each command, a synchronising signal is sent, in this example a wide pulse. After the synchronising signal, a number of time slots are allocated for the code pulses. Each time slot conveys one bit of information: a '1' if there is a pulse present and a '0' if there is no pulse. In the system shown, there are five time slots, each of which can be either '0' or '1', so there are 32 possible code patterns and hence 32 control commands. At the TV receiver, the received pulse pattern is checked for pulses in each of the time slots; the pattern is then decoded as one particular command, which is then executed.

The transmitter unit usually carries a calculator-type keyboard, each key generating a different pulse code. There may be eight to ten channels which can be selected, and other keys are used to control analogue functions such as volume, brightness, and contrast. The analogue functions resemble the simple counter type of channel selection schemes except that the counters can be stepped up or down, causing the volume, etc, to be increased or decreased in steps.

20

What is a SAW filter and how does it work?

A SAW (surface acoustic wave) filter, as its name implies, makes use of ultrasonic waves. It usually has the construction shown in Fig. 13. The filter is built on a plate of piezoelectric material which is able to convert electrical signals into mechanical vibra-

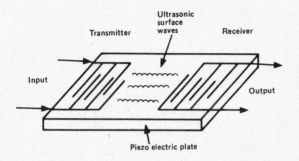

Fig. 13. *Typical SAW filter construction*

tions and vice versa. At one end of the plate, there is a transmitter section consisting of two interleaved comblike electrodes. When an alternating electrical signal is applied across these electrodes, a mechanical vibration is set up in the plate, causing a ripple across the surface of the plate in much the same way as waves ripple across a pond. In a TV IF filter, these waves will have a frequency of 33 to 40 MHz. At the other end of the plate is another pair of comblike electrodes which act as the receiver and convert the mechanical waves back into electrical signals.

The comblike electrodes act very much as do electrical tuned circuits, and their response is governed by the length and spacing of the individual teeth of the combs. By careful design of the electrode geometry, a frequency response like that in Fig. 6 is readily achieved. The SAW device is manufactured by photo-etching techniques similar to those used for integrated circuits, and since the response depends mostly on layout and geometry of the electrodes, it is possible to mass-produce filters which are pre-tuned to the desired frequency response. This type of filter is ideal for use in colour receivers, where the frequency and phase response of the IF must be carefully controlled for good colour reproduction. ·

One disadvantage of SAW filters is that they attenuate the signal somewhat, and a preamplifier stage is required to compensate for losses in the filter.

What is AGC?

In a television receiver, the strength of the received signal can differ from one channel to another, causing variations in picture brightness and contrast. The signals may also be affected by fading resulting from changes in propagation. To overcome these problems, TV receivers are fitted with some form of automatic gain control (AGC).

Most receivers use gated AGC, in which the black level of the video signal is sampled on the back porch of each line-synchronising pulse and a voltage proportional to the black level signal is produced. This control voltage is used to vary the gain of the first IF amplifier stage and the amplifier in the tuner unit, so that if the video level increases, the gain is reduced. This keeps the final video signal more or less constant to give correct contrast and brightness. Usually for weaker signals only, the IF amplifier is controlled, but for large signals, the tuner gain is also reduced. This ensures the best signal-to-noise performance from the tuner unit.

What is AFC?

The frequency of the local oscillator in a TV tuner unit tends to drift with temperature or voltage changes, and this could result in loss of the signal. To overcome this slow drift and make tuning easier, automatic frequency control (AFC) is used.

When the local oscillator is off frequency, the vision carrier presented to the IF amplifier will have a frequency above or below 39.5 MHz. A discriminator circuit in the IF amplifier is used to detect this frequency difference and to produce a control voltage output, as shown in Fig. 14. The control signal is combined with

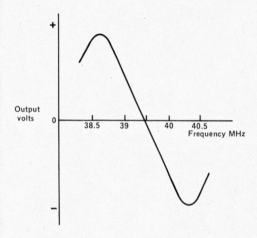

Fig. 14. *Response of AFC discriminator circuit*

the tuning voltage to the tuner unit and causes the oscillator frequency to change until the vision carrier in the IF amplifier becomes 39.5 MHz, when the station will be correctly tuned. Manual tuning is now much easier, since as soon as the oscillator frequency brings the vision carrier within the control range of the AFC discriminator, it will automatically be pulled in to the correct frequency.

What kind of aerial is needed for television reception?

The simplest form of aerial for TV reception is the half-wave dipole shown in Fig. 15. This consists of a metal rod or tube

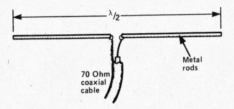

Fig. 15. *A simple dipole TV aerial*

whose length is half a wavelength at the frequency to be received. This can readily be calculated from the formula

$$\text{dipole length} = \frac{150}{f} \text{ metres}$$

where frequency f is in megahertz. Thus a dipole for 600 MHz would have a length of 25 cm.

A dipole is normally cut at the centre, and the signal is taken from each side of the gap as shown. At this point, the dipole presents an impedance of about 70 ohms. To ensure optimum signal transfer, the feeder cable and the TV receiver input should also have an impedance of 70 ohms.

Dipole aerials are usually adequate for reception at ranges up to some 10 miles from a VHF transmitter or 5–6 miles from a UHF transmitter, although this depends on the surrounding terrain: hills and large buildings tend to block the signal if they are in its path, especially at UHF. For reception at greater distance, a multi-element aerial can be used to increase the signal pickup. Perhaps the most popular multi-element type is the Yagi array, named after its Japanese inventor.

Fig. 16 shows a typical three-element Yagi aerial. The centre element is a conventional dipole, and signals from it are fed to the TV receiver. Behind the dipole at a distance of 0.2 wavelength is an element called the 'reflector', which is about 5 per cent longer than the centre dipole. The reflector acts as a short-circuited dipole and re-radiates some of the signal that it picks up. The radiation from the reflector is picked up by the centre dipole and, if the spacing and length of the reflector are correctly chosen, this signal will reinforce that picked up by the dipole itself. The third element is the director, which is 5 per cent shorter than the dipole and spaced about 0.15 wavelength from it. The director acts in much the same way as the reflector, further increasing the signal at the centre element. A typical three-element Yagi will produce about twice the signal of a simple dipole. Adding further directors produces more pickup, but usually only one reflector is used.

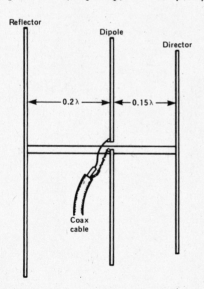

Fig. 16. Typical three-element Yagi aerial

A simple dipole picks up signals equally well from all directions around its axis, as shown in Fig. 17a, but the Yagi aerial has a directional pickup pattern, as shown in Fig. 17. Signal pickup is strong in the direction of the director element and very much reduced from the direction of the reflector. This can be very useful in reducing interference and other unwanted signals. Yagi aerials

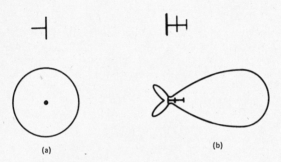

(a)   (b)

Fig. 17. (a) Pickup pattern for a dipole aerial **(b)** Pickup pattern for a Yagi aerial

with more elements give narrower pickup angles and better rejection of signals from the sides and back of the aerial.

Close to he transmitter, it is possible to use indoor set-top aerials. These are usually modified dipoles such as the V or 'rabbit ears' type for VHF; for UHF, a small Yagi aerial is normally used. For the best results, however, the aerial should be out of doors and mounted as high as possible.

What causes ghost images?

One problem with VHF and UHF signals is that they are readily reflected from solid objects such as tall buildings and hills. A reflected signal may be almost as strong as the direct signal, but since it travels over a longer path and radio waves have a finite velocity, the image produced by it is delayed. The result is a ghost image on the screen which appears displaced to the right of the normal picture. The relative phase of the direct and reflected signals also change because of the different path length, so the reflected signal may produce a negative image, in which black has become white and vice versa.

The only cure for ghost image problems is to use a directional aerial and point it so that the reflected signal is reduced relative to the direct signal.

When signals are reflected from an aircraft, the result is a fluttering effect as the direct and reflected signals add to or cancel one another as the path of the reflected signal is changed by the movement of the plane. A similar effect will be noticed when an indoor aerial is used at UHF and people move around in the room, although if the signal is strong, the receiver AGC may be able to take care of these signal changes.

What is aerial polarisation?

When radio signals are transmitted, they are normally either horizontally or vertically polarised according to the direction of the electric field component of the radio wave. From a practical point of view, if the transmitter aerial is a dipole and it is mounted with the rod vertical, then the signal is vertically polarised. If the dipole is horizontal, then the polarisation is horizontal.

If a vertically polarised signal is received on a horizontal aerial, there is considerable loss of signal, so it is important to align the receiving aerial with the same polarisation as the transmitter aerial. For a vertically polarised signal, the elements of a Yagi aerial should be in the vertical plane; for horizontally polarised signals, the elements should be horizontal.

How are satellite TV broadcasts received?

The first requirement for receiving signals from a direct broadcast satellite is a high-gain directional aerial, consisting of a concave dish reflector which acts like a mirror collecting the signal and focusing it on to a small horn-type pickup aerial mounted in front of the dish. For a home installation the dish, made of aluminium or aluminium-coated fibreglass, is about 0.7 metre diameter.

A typical system for reception of satellites is shown in Figure 18. Signals picked up by the horn are amplified by a special low-noise amplifier (LNA), using gallium arsenide (GaAs) field effect transistors. The amplified signals are mixed with a local oscillator to produce an IF in the UHF band (500–900 MHz), where further amplification is carried out. This part of the system is usually mounted on the dish aerial.

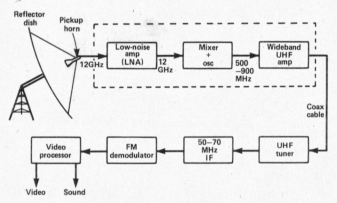

Fig. 18. *Typical satellite receiver system*

A modified UHF tuner converts the UHF signal to an IF of 50–70 MHz and an FM demodulator is used to extract the vision and sound signals. Note that all satellite transmissions use frequency modulation for the vision signal.

The video and sound signals may be fed directly to a TV monitor or to a UHF modulator, which produces an aerial input signal for a standard TV receiver. Some transmissions for cable or subscription channels may be 'scrambled', and subscribers will have a video processor unit to decode the signals so that the programmes can be viewed.

3
Video displays

How is a television picture displayed?

Television pictures are almost always displayed by using a picture tube which is a development of the cathode ray tube used in oscilloscopes and radar displays.

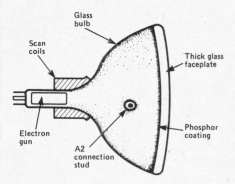

Fig. 19. Basic construction of a TV picture tube

Fig. 19 shows the basic construction of a television picture tube. The envelope of the tube is normally of glass, although some tubes with metal cones have been made, and consists of a narrow cylindrical neck which flares out into a cone, to end in an approximately flat faceplate on which the picture is displayed. The whole tube is pumped and sealed to leave a vacuum inside.

In the neck of the tube is an electron-gun assembly, which produces a finely focussed beam of electrons. The electrons are aimed at a material called 'phosphor' which covers the inside of the faceplate and forms the screen on which the picture is produced. When struck by the beam of electrons, the phosphor glows to produce a spot of light whose brightness depends on the intensity of the beam.

To build up a picture, the electron beam must be scanned over the screen in a series of horizontal lines in the same way that the televised scene was scanned. If the video signal is used to modulate the intensity of the electron beam, a pattern of light and shade will be produced on the screen to form the required picture. This scanning process is controlled by two sets of coils mounted on the neck of the tube.

How is the electron beam produced?

A typical electron gun is shown in Fig. 20. A heated, barium oxide coated, cathode emits a stream of electrons which are accelerated along the tube in the direction of the screen by a high positive potential on the anode electrode (A2). This anode consists of a cylinder in the neck of the tube and is extended as a conductive coating on the inside of the glass envelope to within an inch or so of the screen. Typical voltages applied to the A2 anode are from 10 000 V to perhaps 25 000 V, depending on the screen size. To avoid internal flash-over, the high-voltage connection is made to the coating through a recessed stud in the glass cone of the tube, and the connecting lead is covered by a rubber cap to prevent corona discharge.

A grid electrode is mounted in front of the cathode and used to control the intensity of the beam and hence the spot brightness. The name 'grid' comes from valve terminology, but in practice this electrode is a cylindrical cap with a hole in the end to allow the electron beam to pass through. When the grid is made negative relative to the cathode, it tends to repel some of the electrons and reduce the number passing through to form the beam. As the negative bias is increased, the beam intensity falls and the spot on the screen becomes dimmer until eventually the beam is completely cut off.

The fourth elecrode is anode A1, which is used to focus the beam of electrons and is often called the 'focus anode'. If an electron beam passes through an electric field, it will be bent towards the positive side of the field. By careful design of the shape and spacing of A1 and A2 and the voltages applied to them, an electric field can be set up which acts like a lens and deflects the electrons in the beam so that they all meet at a single point on the screen to produce a sharply focussed dot. Adjustment of the voltage applied to anode A1 allows fine ajustments of the focussing.

Most modern television tubes use the four-electrode (tetrode) gun, but some earlier tubes use a triode structure with only one anode. In these tubes, focussing of the electron beam is by means of a magnetic field produced by an external magnet assembly on the neck of the tube. A mechanical adjustment which alters the

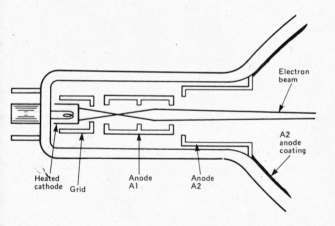

Fig. 20. Sectional view of the electron gun of a tetrode picture tube

shape and strength of the magnetic field is used for fine control of focussing.

How is the electron beam scanned over the screen?

When a beam of electrons passes through a magnetic field, it will be deflected at right angles to the field by an amount depending on the strength and polarity of the field. Modern television tubes invariably use magnetic fields to scan the beam across and down the screen to produce the picture.

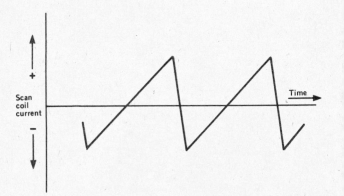

Fig. 21. Current waveform in the scan coils

Four deflection coils on an iron or ferrite yoke are mounted around the neck of the tube to provide the deflection fields. One pair of coils above and below the neck produces a vertical magnetic field which will sweep the spot from side to side on the screen when a current is passed through them. A second set of coils at each side of the tube neck produces a horizontal magnetic field, and currents in these coils will move the beam up and down the screen.

32

To produce the required linear scanning action, the scan coils are driven by a current which has a sawtooth waveform, as shown in Fig. 21. The linearly rising current provides the scan across the screen, while the rapid current reversal at the end of the scan produces a rapid retrace ready for the start of the next scan. Typical values for the scan current are 500 mA to 1 A peak to peak.

For the vertical scan system, a circuit similar to that shown in Fig. 22 is used. A sawtooth voltage waveform is produced by

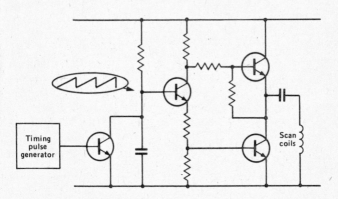

Fig. 22. Simplified version of vertical scan driver circuit

charging a capacitor through a large resistor to produce the linear part of the scan. At the end of the scan, a pulse from the timing generator turns on a transistor across the capacitor, and this provides a rapid discharge for the retrace. The current through the coils is produced by a circuit similar to an audio amplifier. The inductance of the coils has some effect on the current waveform, so feedback and waveshaping circuits are usually added to linearise the scan waveform. The vertical height of the picture is governed by the amplitude of the current and is controlled in much the same way as volume on an audio amplifier.

In the horizontal scan circuits, where the scanning rate is very much higher (typically, 15 kHz), the inductance of the scan coils has much more effect, and the voltage waveform to the coils is almost a square wave. In the line-scan circuits, the drive transistor merely acts as a switch which is triggered by a timing oscillator. The coils are usually driven through a transformer, and the width of the picture is controlled by some form of variable inductance in series with the coils.

How is the high voltage for the tube produced?

The high voltage supply for the picture-tube anode is generated by using the back EMF produced across the line scan coils when the magnetic field reverses at the end of the scan. At this time, the rapidly changing magnetic field generates a back EMF of several hundred volts across the scan coils and the transformer winding. By adding an extra winding to the scan transformer, as shown in Fig. 23, the pulse of voltage can be stepped up to several thousand

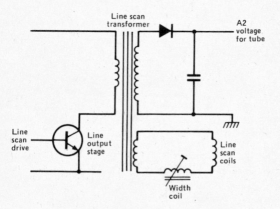

Fig. 23. *Part of line-scan output circuits, showing EHT generation and width control*

volts and is rectified by a diode and used to charge a capacitor. Since the frequency of the pulses is high, the capacitor need have a capacitance of only 1000 pF or so to maintain its charge between pulses. In most tubes, this capacitor is formed between the internal A2 coating and an external graphite coating on the tube itself, the glass of the envelope acting as the capacitor.

For higher voltages, a voltage doubler or tripler may be used from the transformer overwinding.

What is an aluminised screen and why is it used?

The phosphor used for the screen coating of a picture tube is a relatively poor conductor. When it is bombarded by the electron beam, some areas of the screen will acquire a negative charge, which tends to slow down the beam before it hits the screen and reduce the brightness of the picture at those points. A thin aluminium coating on the rear surface of the screen overcomes this problem. At the same time, the aluminium reflects light from the rear of the screen forwards, thus increasing still further the brilliance of the picture.

How is synchronisation achieved?

In order to reproduce the received picture correctly, it is essential that the scanning process in the picture tube is exactly synchronised to the incoming video signal. This is achieved by making use of the synchronisation pulses which form part of the video signal.

The synchronising pulses are separated from the picture information by a circuit similar to that shown in Fig. 24. An inverted video signal is used so that the sync pulse tips are positive going. Transistor TR1 is biassed so that it will conduct during the sync pulses but is cut off during the picture part of the signal. As a result, only the sync pulses will appear at its collector, as shown in Fig. 25.

The field pulses are much wider than the line pulses and are separated out by using an integrator circuit consisting of a series

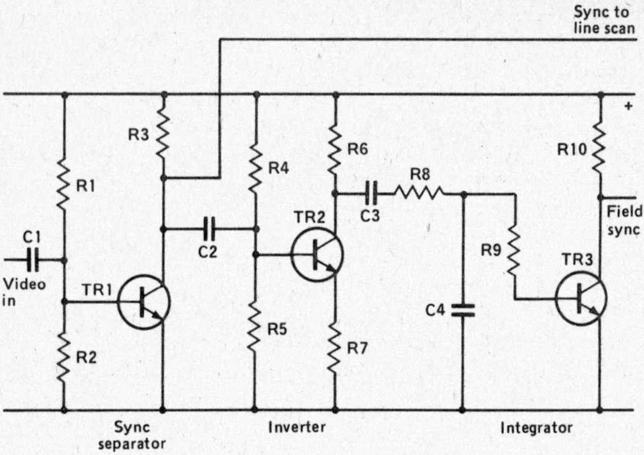

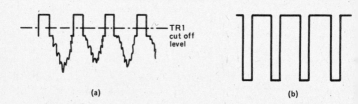

Fig. 24. Typical sync separation circuit

Fig. 25. Action of sync separator stage. **(a)** Input waveform. **(b)** Waveform at collector of TR1

36

resistor feeding a capacitor. During the short line pulses, the capacitor does not have time to charge, but when the field pulses come along, they charge the capacitor to form a rather rounded pulse which is amplified and squared up by the amplifier stage TR3. Transistor TR2 merely inverts the signal to ensure that the field pulses are of the right polarity to drive the integrator and TR3. The waveforms for this part of the circuit are shown in Fig. 26.

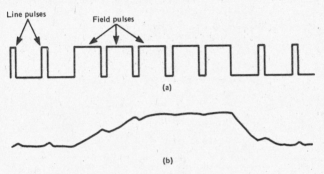

Fig. 26. Action of the integrator in separating field pulses. **(a)** Voltage waveform at collector of TR2. **(b)** Voltage waveform across C4

The field scan timing generator is normally set so that it runs a little more slowly than the correct scan rate. The field sync pulse is then applied to trigger a new scan to bring the field scan into step with the received signal. For the line-scan, direct triggerng can produce ragged edges to the picture because of noise on the received signal, so a different approach, known as 'flywheel synchronisation', is used. Here the timing of the line-scan retrace and the line sync pulses are compared, and a control voltage proportional to the timing error is generated. This control signal is used to correct the timing of the line-scan generator until it is in step with the sync pulses. Any disturbances due to noise are corrected out over several scan-lines and produce little effect on the picture.

37

What is the difference between a television receiver and a video monitor?

Unlike television receivers, most video monitors are designed to run from a direct video input, although a few of the more sophisticated monitors contain a receiver section. The typical input to a video monitor is a video signal of about 1 V peak amplitude.

Video monitors are built to a much higher standard of engineering than domestic receivers; they usually come in a metal case, often with facilities for mounting them into an equipment rack. The picture tube for a monitor is designed to give a smaller spot size and more accurate focussing over the whole screen, and the scan circuits are designed for better linearity and rock-steady pictures. Video circuits in a monitor are usually designed to handle a wider bandwidth signal than those in a TV set, since the input signal is unaffected by the limitations of the receiver system.

Colour monitors may have either a composite colour video input, or separate red, green, and blue inputs.

How are large screen pictures produced?

To obtain pictures on screens up to perhaps 8 ft. by 6 ft., a projection system is used. A small picture tube of 2 in. to 5 in. diameter is used, operating with an extremely bright image on its screen. By a system of lenses or mirrors, the image is projected on to the screen like a cinema film or a slide.

The usual arrangement for a projector is the Schmidt type of mirror system shown in Fig. 27. The image on the tube is focussed on a concave silvered mirror. The light rays from the concave mirror are bent at right angles by a plane mirror to avoid the obstruction that would be presented by the tube and its scan coils. The light finally passes through a corrector plate to cancel out optical distortion produced by the spherical shape of the concave mirror. In most projection systems, the face of the tube itself is also specially curved to reduce optical distortion of the picture.

To achieve a very bright image, the projection tube operates with a very high acceleration voltage (typically, 30 kV to 50 kV).

Because of the high energy of the electron beam, X-rays are usually produced, and so it is unwise to view this type of tube directly without some form of eye protection.

Colour systems use three projection units, and the tubes have red, green, and blue phosphors to produce three coloured images which are then superimposed on the screen.

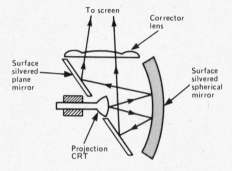

Fig. 27. *Sectional view of Schmidt-type projector*

4
Colour television

What is colour?

Light consists of electromagnetic waves with a very much higher frequency, or very much shorter wavelength, than radio waves. Visible light covers a range of wavelengths from about 400 nm to about 700 nm. Colour is determined by the particular wavelengths of light present. At the 700 nm wavelength, light is red; colour changes through orange, yellow, and green to blue and violet as the wavelengths get shorter. White light is produced when wavelengths throughout the visible band are present at the same time. This can be demonstrated by passing white light through a prism, when the various wavelengths and hence the colours of the spectrum are spread out as shown in Fig. 28.

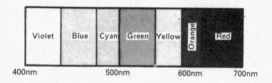

Fig. 28. The spectrum of white light

For television and photography, it was found that light of any colour could be produced by adding together various proportions of red, green, and blue light. When these three colours, known as the 'additive' primary colours, are added together equally, white light is produced.

40

If red and green light are combined, the result is yellow light. This can also be looked on as white light from which the blue component has been subtracted. Similarly, magenta and cyan (a bluish green) can be produced by subtracting green or red light respectively from white. Yellow, magenta, and cyan are known as the 'subtractive' primaries or 'complementary' colours.

What are hue and saturation?

'Hue' is the basic colour of light – red, orange, yellow, green, and so on.

'Saturation' is the colourfulness of the light. A pure red light is fully saturated. As the degree of saturation is reduced, the red light becomes dark pink, then pale pink, and finally, with no saturation, all trace of colour will disappear, leaving a shade of grey. Saturation is normally measured in percentages.

How is a colour-television picture produced?

In a colour-television camera, the red, green, and blue components of the light from the scene being televised are separated out

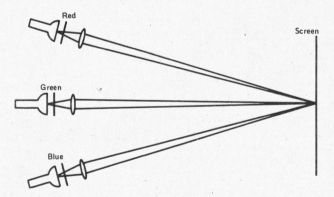

Fig. 29. Principle of a colour television display using three projectors

by colour filters. These three images are then converted into three separate video signals for the red, green, and blue parts of the total image.

At the display end, three picture tubes are used and are fed with the red, green, and blue video signals respectively. The red tube is fitted with a red filter so that it produces a red image, and so on. When all three pictures from the tubes are superimposed, they merge to give a full-colour image of the televised scene. This is shown in Fig. 29.

This three-tube technique is commonly used for colour projection systems, but for domestic television a direct-view tube of the shadowmask type is normally used. In this system, three coloured images are generated and combined in a single tube.

How does a shadowmask colour tube work?

The original shadowmask tube for colour television was developed by RCA and is in effect three tubes in one, as shown in Fig. 30. Three separate electron guns are mounted in the neck of

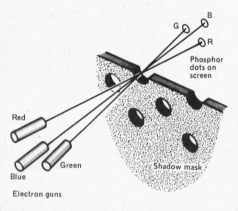

Fig. 30. Basic arrangement of a delta-gun shadowmask tube

the tube in a triangular layout. Because of this arrangement of the guns, this type of tube is often referred to as a 'delta gun' tube. One of the three guns is driven by the red video signal, the others by green and blue respectively.

Instead of the normal continuous phosphor coating, the screen consists of an array of tiny phosphor dots arranged in groups of three. A group consists of red, green, and blue dots arranged in a triangular pattern to match the layout of the three electron guns. Between the screen and the guns is a steel shadowmask which contains a pattern of tiny holes, one for each group of dots on the screen. The holes in the mask are aligned relative to the dots on the screen and to the electron guns so that the beam from the red gun passing through a hole in the mask will fall on a red dot on the screen, while the green and blue beams passing through the same hole will hit green and blue dots respectively.

When video signals are applied, the red gun gives a red image on the screen, while the green and blue guns produce green and blue images, which are combined with the red one. Since the dots are very tiny and close together, the viewer is unable to resolve individual dots and his eye will merge the three images together to form a composite colour picture.

What is convergence?

One problem with a delta-gun shadowmask colour tube is to ensure that the three beams pass through the holes in the mask at the proper angle to hit the correct dots. Normally, all three beams are deflected by a common scanning field, and because of the geometry of the tube and the layout of the guns, a technique known as 'convergence' is needed to keep the three beams aligned with dots of the correct colours.

Convergence is achieved by a magnetic convergence yoke mounted on the neck of the tube near the thre guns, as shown in Fig. 31. A magnet on each polepiece is adjusted to move the mean position of its beam. This process is known as 'static convergence' and takes into account the alignment of the guns themselves.

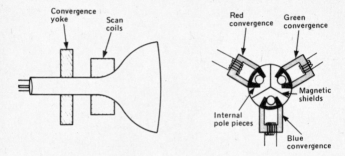

Fig. 31. Convergence coils and yoke for a delta-gun tube

As the beams are scanned across and down the screen, a series of dynamic corrections is needed to keep them aligned with the mask and dots. Signals derived from the line and field scanning circuits are applied to coils on the convergence yoke. This is known as 'dynamic convergence'. When the convergence is misaligned, severe colour distortion can occur, but by careful adjustment of the static and dynamic convergence, the beams can be properly aligned over most of the screen area to give perfectly acceptable colour pictures.

What is an in-line tube and why is it used?

In delta-gun tubes, convergence of the three beams is a complicated process. Most of the newer types of tube use an in-line arrangment of the guns, where they are mounted in a horizontal line across the neck of the tube. The screen of such a tube has vertical phosphor stripes rather than dots, and the shadowmask has a set of vertical slits instead of holes. The general arrangement of such a tube is as shown in Fig. 32.

The basic operation of an in-line tube is similar to that of the ordinary shadowmask type, but because the guns are in a horizontal line, the convergence problem is very much simpler.

Some in-line tubes have the deflection and convergence yokes aligned and cemented to the tubes when they are made, thus simplifying still further the adjustments needed in the television receiver. Typical tubes of this type are the 20AX and 30AX types from Mullard.

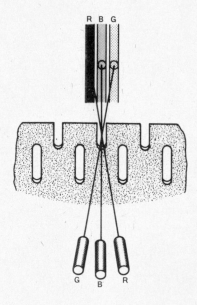

Fig. 32. Principle of a precision in-line gun tube with slotted mask and striped screen

An added advantage of the in-line gun and slotted mask system is that less of the electron beam needs to be masked off to ensure correct colour registration. As a result, the screen image in this type of tube is usually brighter than in a delta-gun tube.

What is degaussing and why is it needed?

In a colour tube, the shadowmask is normally made of some form of steel to ensure strength and rigidity. The steel may become permanently magnetised by external magnetic fields near the receiver. If this occurs, the mask itself will tend to deflect the electron beams as they pass through it, causing them to land on the wrong phosphor dots and producing colour errors over parts of the picture. This problem is dealt with by using degaussing coils.

The degaussing coils are mounted, one on each side, over the flared cone of the picture tube. When a current is passed through them, they produce a magnetic field through the tube, its shadowmask, and the surrounding metalwork. Each time the set is switched on, an alternating current is passed through the degaussing coils, producing an alternating magnetic field which effectively removes any permanent magnetism in the tube and surrounding metal parts. After a few seconds, the coil current is slowly reduced to zero, leaving the tube completely demagnetised.

What is the luminance signal?

In a colour-television system, the luminance signal, usually denoted by the symbol Y, is a video signal which represents the image of the televised scene in terms of brightness only. It is the signal that would be produced by a monochrome camera.

A colour camera normally produces three video outputs representing the red (R), green (G), and blue (B) light from the scene. The luminance signal Y is obtained by combining these in the proportions $Y = 0.3R + 0.59G + 0.11B$.

These values are chosen to match fairly closely the response of the human eye and should produce the proper grey tones on a monochrome receiver.

If R, G, and B are all at 100 per cent, then Y is also 100 per cent, and this represents white. If R, G, and B are equal but less than 100 per cent, then Y has the same value and will represent a shade of grey which gets darker as the value of Y falls until it becomes black at $Y = 0$.

What is the chrominance signal?

As well as luminance, the colour television system also needs signals representing the colour of the image. These are called the 'chrominance signals'. They can be derived by simply subtracting the Y signal from each of the R, G, and B signals to give three colour difference signals $R\text{-}Y$, $G\text{-}Y$, and $B\text{-}Y$.

When there is no colour, R, G, B, and Y are all equal, and the colour difference signals will all cancel out to zero. A colour receiver in these conditions will respond only to luminance and gives the same display as a monochrome receiver.

In practice, only the $R\text{-}Y$ and $B\text{-}Y$ components actually need to be transmitted with the Y signal. The third signal $G\text{-}Y$ can readily be derived from $R\text{-}Y$, $B\text{-}Y$, and Y at the receiver.

The $R\text{-}Y$ and $B\text{-}Y$ signals are modified slightly in amplitude before they are transmitted.

What is NTSC?

The first practical colour-television system to be used for regular broadcasting was the American NTSC (National Television System Committee) system, which was developed in the early 1950s. The main objectives were a system which would be compatible with existing monochrome receivers and would fit into the existing television-channel bandwidth.

A luminance (Y) signal is transmitted which is virtually identical to the older monochrome signal and so ensures compatibility with existing black-and-white receivers.

For colour signals, it was found that the human eye was unable to resolve fine details in colour and that a bandwidth of only some 1 MHz would be adequate for colour information. The $R\text{-}Y$ and $B\text{-}Y$ chrominance informaton is transmitted on a subcarrier of approximately 3.58 MHz, using quadrature amplitude modulation and a suppressed carrier.

Quadrature amplitude modulation means that the $R\text{-}Y$ signal is modulated on to a subcarrier signal which is 90 deg. out of phase with the subcarrier used for $B\text{-}Y$. When the two subcarrier signals are combined, they produce a single signal whose phase, relative to say the *B-Y* subcarrier phase, varies with the ratio of the *R-Y* and *B-Y* signals as shown in Fig. 33. The result is that the hue of the colour is determined by the phase of the combined signal and colour saturation by its amplitude, as shown in Fig. 34.

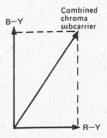

Fig. 33. *Addition of two subcarriers at 90 degree phase angle to produce final chrominance signal*

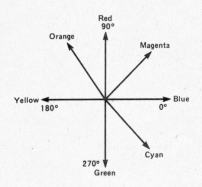

Fig. 34. *Effect of phase of combined subcarrier on hue*

48

To avoid annoying patterning on monochrome receivers, the 3.58 MHz subcarrier is suppressed, leaving only the sideband components, which contain the required chrominance data. This signal is added to the luminance and sound subcarrier signals before modulation on to a radio frequency carrier for transmission. Fig. 35 shows the layout of the luminance, chrominance, and sound signals within the television channel for the PAL system.

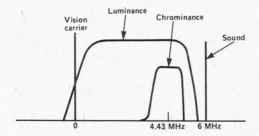

Fig. 35. Components of a British PAL TV signal relative to the vision carrier frequency

What is the reference burst and why is it needed?

When the quadrature modulated suppressed carrier chrominance signal is received, two requirements must be met before it can be demodulated and resolved into separate colour signals.

First, in order to demodulate the signal, a locally generated carrier signal must be produced with exactly the same frequency as the suppressed subcarrier.

Second, if the $R-Y$ and $B-Y$ components are to be sorted out from the combined signal, the phase of the local carrier must be the same as, say, the original $B-Y$ carrier at the transmitter.

To achieve these objectives, some form of reference must be transmitted. This is done by inserting a short burst of about ten cycles of subcarrier frequency during the blanking after each line-synchronisation pulse, as shown in Fig. 36. This reference burst might have the same phase as the *B-Y* subcarrier, and the locally generated signal can be locked to it in both frequency and phase to give correct demodulation and separation of the colour signals.

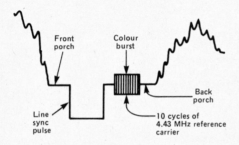

Fig. 36. *Position of the reference burst on the back porch of line sync pulses*

One major problem with the NTSC system is that the phase of the chrominance signals can vary from one station to another; it can also be affected when the signal is passed over a network or recorded and played back from a videotape. At the receiver, signal fading and temperature changes can affect the phase of the locally generated subcarrier relative to the colour burst. All these effects will produce changes in the hue of the colours on the screen. Receivers normally have a hue control by which the phase of the subcarrier generator can be altered, and this is adjusted by the viewer to produce acceptable colour.

Alternative colour television systems, such as SECAM and PAL, have been devised to overcome these problems. In the USA, where NTSC is still used, a special colour-reference signal is now transmitted during the field-blanking interval, and some of the newer receivers use this to automatically correct hue errors.

What are SECAM and PAL?

In an attempt to overcome the problems of hue variation caused by changes in phase of the NTSC chrominance signals, a new system called SECAM (sequential colour and memory) has been developed in France.

In the SECAM system, the R-Y and B-Y chrominance signals are transmitted separately on alternate scan lines. Frequency modulation of a 4.43 MHz subcarrier is used. No colour-burst pulses are used, but at the start of each field scan, a series of identification signals is sent so that the receiver will be able to determine which lines carry the R-Y signal and which carry the B-Y.

In the receiver, a delay line is used to delay chrominance signals by exactly one line scan period. On one scan line the received B-Y signal is combined with a delayed R-Y signal from the previous scan line. On the next scan, the direct R-Y is combined with a delayed B-Y, and so on. Switching between the direct and delayed signals is controlled by the line-scan and is synchronised by the identification signals at the start of each field.

PAL (phase alternation line) is a system developed by Telefunken in Germany; like NTSC, it uses suppressed carrier-quadrature modulation. The key difference is that in PAL the phase of the R-Y signal is reversed on alternate scan-lines.

In the PAL receiver, a delay line similar to that in the SECAM system is used. The direct and delayed signals from a pair of successive scan-lines are then combined to produce the colour outputs. Any phase errors in transmission tend to be cancelled out because of the alternating phase of the R-Y signal.

Like NTSC, the PAL system uses a colour reference burst on each scan-line, and the phase of this changes through 90 deg. on alternate scans. This phase swing is used to identify the R-Y phase for each scan-line.

Because they operate on pairs of scan-lines, the SECAM and PAL systems give only half the vertical colour resolution, but this is perfectly adequate on a 625-line system. No hue controls are needed in receivers for these systems, since any phase changes are either cancelled or have no effect on hue.

The three systems are incompatible with one another, so a PAL receiver will not work with either NTSC or SECAM. Some receivers are built which can be switched to work with any of the three systems and with 525 or 625 lines.

How does a PAL decoder work?

Fig. 37 shows the basic arrangement of a PAL decoder.

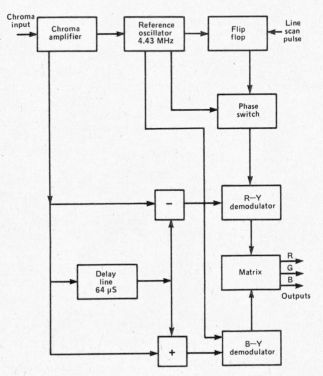

Fig. 37. Simplified block diagram of a PAL colour decoder

52

Chrominance signals are separated from the luminance by a high pass filter and then pass through a chrominance amplifier. Part of this amplifier provides automatic chroma control (ACC), which varies the gain to keep the reference burst at a preset amplitude. A manual gain control allows the level of colour saturation to be controlled.

The local subcarrier generator is a crystal controlled oscillator running at 4.43 MHz which is phase-locked to the colour-burst signal on each scan line.

Chrominance signals are passed through a delay line and then combined with the direct chrominance signal. B-Y signals are obtained by adding the direct and delayed signals when the alternate phase R-Y signals cancel out. The R-Y signals can be obtained by subtracting the direct and delayed signals so that the B-Y signals cancel and the R-Y signals add together. These sum and difference signals are then fed to the B-Y and R-Y demodulators.

A flipflop circuit driven from the line-scan pulses is used to switch the phase of the subcarrier signal to the R-Y demodulator on alternate scan lines to produce the correct R-Y output. A signal from the reference-oscillator phase lock circuits is used to ensure that the flipflop switches in the correct sequence.

Finally the Y, R-Y, and B-Y signals are fed to a matrix circuit from which the R, G, and B drives for the display tube are derived.

When no colour is being transmitted, there will be no R-Y or B-Y signals and no burst pulse. Since the local subcarrier generator is still running, the colour circuits could respond to noise and produce speckles or patches of colour on the screen. To avoid this, a 'colour killer' circuit is used. This detects the 7.8 kHz signal produced by the changing phase of the colour burst and, if this is not present, the chrominance amplifier is turned off to prevent noise or other signals from reaching the colour demodulators.

Although in early PAL and SECAM receivers, the colour decoder section was very complex, a modern receiver has just one or two integrated circuits and a few other components to perform this function.

What is grey scale tracking?

In a colour-display tube, the three guns and the three colour phosphors will each have a different response to the colour-drive signals. Unless these characteristics are matched, there will be some colour bias in either the highlight or shadow areas of the picture.

Basically, two adjustments are required. These are usually carried out when the tube is displaying a monochrome pattern consisting of a series of brightness steps ranging from black through various greys to white.

To set up the shadow areas, the cutoff points of the three guns must be adjusted so that they all cut off at the picture-black level. This is done by adjusting the bias on each gun individually.

For the highlight areas of the picture, the video drive to each gun is adjusted until all three guns produce the same brightness on the screen for white or light-grey colours.

Usually, these two adjustments interact with one another, so it is necessary to make them alternately until the correct results are obtained. Bias is adjusted to remove any colour bias in dark-grey areas, while the drive is set to remove any colour bias in the light-grey areas of the picture.

5
Video cameras

How does a video camera work?

Optically, a home video camera is similar to a home movie camera except that the light-sensitive target electrode of a vidicon camera tube takes the place of the photographic film. The general arrangement is shown in Fig. 38.

A lens is used to focus an image of the scene which is being televised on to the photoelectric target of the vidicon tube. This target converts the light levels of the image into electrical signals and is scanned electronically to generate the required video signal.

The small signals from the vidicon tube are amplified to a level of about 0.7 V peak, and a sequence of line and field synchronising pulses is added to produce a composite video output signal. These line and field pulses are produced by a synchronising pulse generator (SPG) and are also used to control the scanning circuits for the camera tube.

To enable the operator to see what is being televised, a viewfinder is fitted to the camera. On simple cameras, this is usually an optical telescope device mounted on top of the camera body and adjusted to give a view similar to that seen by the lens. This type of finder has two main disadvantages. First, if the lens is changed for another of different focal length, the viewfinder also needs to be changed to present the correct view. Second, because the viewfinder is not on the same axis as the lens, it shows a slightly different view of the scene; this is particularly noticeable on closeup shots.

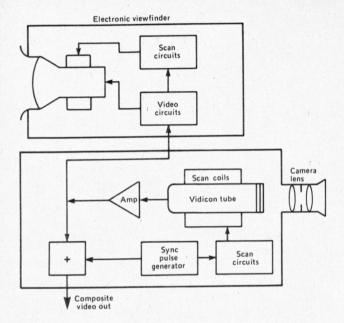

Fig. 38. Block diagram of video camera with an electronic viewfinder

More sophisticated cameras use either an optical reflex viewfinder or an electronic viewfinder. In the reflex type, the image in the viewfinder is taken from the camera lens by a series of mirrors and prisms and shows the view actually being seen by the lens. For an electronic viewfinder, the video signal from the camera tube is used to drive a small monitor with, say, a 2 in. picture tube, and this shows the actual picture being produced by the camera tube.

Sound may be picked up by a microphone mounted on a boom from the top of the camera and amplified by an audio amplifier inside the camera body. Alternatively, sound may be dealt with by an entirely separate audio system.

Most home video cameras provide separate sound and video output signals which can be fed to either a video monitor or a videotape recorder. Some cameras also have a UHF modulator built in which produces a combined sound and vision signal at UHF which is similar to a normal TV broadcast. This signal can be fed to the aerial input of a TV receiver or tape recorder.

What is the photoconductive effect?

Certain materials, such as cadmium sulphide, have the property of changing their electrical conductivity when they are exposed to light. This is known as the 'photoconductive effect' and is the principle used in vidicon camera tubes to convert a light image into an electrical signal.

A typical photoconductive cell, such as those used for photographic exposure meters, has the structure shown in Fig. 39. A

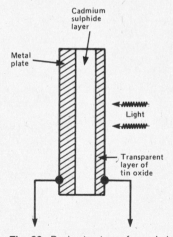

Fig. 39. Basic structure of a cadmium sulphide photocell

layer of cadmium sulphide is sandwiched between two metal electrodes. In order to allow the light to reach the cadmium sulphide layer, one electrode is either an open mesh grid or a very thin transparent layer of tin oxide.

In total darkness, cadmium sulphide is a poor conductor, and if a voltage is applied across the cell, very little current will flow through the circuit. This current is called the 'dark' current.

When light falls on the cell, some of the energy in the light waves is transferred to the electrons within the atoms of cadmium sulphide. Some of these electrons will attain an energy level sufficient to allow them to break free of their parent atoms and diffuse through the cadmium sulphide layer. These free electrons act as charge carriers and cause an effective increase in the conductivity of the sulphide layer. When a voltage is now applied to the cell, appreciable current will flow. The conductivity and hence the current are roughly proportional to the intensity of light falling on the cell.

How does a vidicon tube work?

The most popular type of camera tube for use in home video cameras is the vidicon, whose construction is shown in Fig. 40.

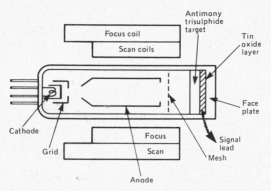

Fig. 40. Construction of a typical vidicon camera tube

At one end of the tube is a flat glass faceplate, behind which is the photoconductive target electrode. This target is made from a layer of antimony trisulphide, and it is separated from the faceplate by a transparent layer of tin oxide, which acts as a contact electrode.

An electron gun, similar to the type used in a picture tube, is mounted at the other end of the vidicon tube and is used to focus a beam of electrons on to the rear face of the target electrode. Coils mounted on the neck of the vidicon provide magnetic fields for focussing the beam and scanning it across the target. At the target end of the electron gun, a mesh electrode slows down the beam before it reaches the target, effectively stabilising the potential at the rear face of the target at the same level as at the cathode of the electron gun.

When an image is focussed on the target by the camera lens, the conductivity through the target layer will change from point to point according to the pattern of light on the face of the target. The target can be imagined as a vast array of tiny resistors packed side by side, each resistor running from the front to the back of the target. The value of an individual resistor depends on the intensity of the light falling on the target at that point in the array.

When the electron beam strikes the rear of the target, it effectively completes the circuit through a tiny element of the target, and a current flows according to the intensity of light falling on that element. As the beam is scanned over the target, the current varies in sympathy with changes in the light level to produce a video signal across the external load resistor.

What is lag and how does it affect a vidicon tube?

When light has been falling on a photoconductor for a time and is then cut off, the current in the circuit does not fall immediately to the dark level but dies away slowly. This effect is called 'lag' and can cause problems in a vidicon camera tube.

If the camera is pointed at a background and a moving object passes in front, an image of the background may show through the moving object, giving it a ghostlike quality. If a bright light appears in the scene and moves across the field of view, it will be followed by a 'comet tail' as the image on the photoconductive target dies away. Modern vidicons have specially designed electron guns and improved targets intended to minimise these effects, but they are always present to some extent.

A further problem with vidicons is 'burn-in' where the tube has had a very bright image on it for some time. The image may be retained on the target for a long time, and in extreme cases permenent damage may be caused to the vidicon tube.

What other types of camera tube are used?

One type of tube which is particularly suited to colour cameras is the plumbicon, which has the same basic construction as a vidicon but uses a target based on a lead oxide material. This type of tube is much more sensitive than a vidicon type and is much less affected by lag and burn-in problems.

Other target materials have been used, such as cadmium selenide in the Toshiba Chalnicon tube and zinc selenide in the Newvicon tube. Both of these are similar to the vidicon, but their higher light sensitivity makes them useful in low light levels.

Special camera tubes for very low light levels use a silicon target and often include intensifier devices to allow pictures to be obtained when the human eye cannot detect an image. Such cameras are used for special applications such as military surveillance and are unlikely to be found in home video equipment.

What kind of lens is used on a video camera?

Most home video cameras use a 17 mm diameter camera tube which gives an image similar in size to that on a 16 mm movie film. As a result, many simple cameras use interchangeable lenses based on 16 mm cine lenses. Broadcasting studio cameras tend to use the larger 25 mm diameter camera tube and lenses which are similar to those on professional 35 mm movie cameras.

60

For a 17 mm vidicon system, the standard lens usually has a focal length of about 25 mm, giving a horizontal angle of view of 20 to 25 deg. A telephoto lens with 75 mm focal length gives a narrower angle of view and produces a closeup view of more distant objects. For wide-angle views, a lens of perhaps 12 mm focal length could be used. For security systems, where a very wide angle of view may be desirable, an extra-wide-angle lens such as the 'fish eye' type might be used, although such lenses produce a considerably distorted picture.

Like home movie cameras, many video cameras are fitted with a zoom lens whose effective focal length can be varied over a range of perhaps 6 to 1 by simply operating a lever on the lens barrel. This type of lens is particularly useful at sports events, where the view can be changed rapidly from a wide-angle shot of the playing field to a closeup of a particular player merely by operating the zoom control on the lens.

All modern lenses contain a number of glass elements designed to correct various faults that can occur in a simple lens. To reduce internal reflections and improve the contrast and brightness of the image, the individual elements normally have a thin anti-reflective coating.

What do the 'f' numbers on a lens mean?

Like the human eye, all camera lenses contain an iris or diaphragm to control the amount of light passing through the lens and thus the brightness of the image it produces. This iris is adjusted by rotating a ring on the lens barrel.

Iris settings are normally marked with f numbers, such as $f4$, $f5.6$, $f8$, and so on. The f number is the ratio between the focal length of the lens and the effective diameter of the aperture in the iris. Thus a 25 mm focal length lens with its iris at $f4$ will have an aperture diameter of about 6 mm.

Image brightness is proportional to the area of the iris aperture, so if the f number changes from $f4$ to $f2$, the diameter is doubled and the brightness is increased by a factor of four. The f numbers are usually arranged in a sequence in which each number is 1.4

times the previous one (i.e., $f2$, $f2.8$, $f4$, etc.), so each step doubles the image brightness.

Lenses are often specified by their maximum aperture or lowest f number, since this indicates the performance of the lens in low light conditions. Thus an $f2$ lens is more useful in low light conditions than an $f4$ lens.

What is depth of field?

A camera lens normally has a focus control marked in distances of either feet or metres. This control enables the lens to be focussed sharply on an object at the set distance. At other distances, the sharpness of the image will gradually fall off, but there will be a range on each side of the sharp-focus point where the image is acceptably sharp. This range is called the 'depth of field' of the lens.

Depth of field is affected by the aperture setting of the lens, being greatest with the smallest aperture (highest f number) and least at the full aperture of the lens. The focal length of the lens also affects depth of field, short focal lengths giving maximum depth of field and long focal lengths giving shallow depth of field. This characteristic can be used to pick out an object from the background by focussing a telephoto lens at wide aperture on the object, which will stand out in sharp focus against a blurred background.

How are sync pulses generated?

A simple sync pulse generator (SPG) for a video camera might be arranged as shown in Fig. 41. A primary clock oscillator generates a square wave at twice the line-scan frequency. This clock is fed to a divide-by-two circuit to produce line-scan frequency, and this is used to trigger a short-pulse generator for the line sync pulses.

The clock is also fed to a divider chain consisting of four divide-by-five stages to give a total division ratio of 625. The output of this counter chain produces a pulse every $312\frac{1}{2}$ lines and can be used to drive a pulse-generator circuit to produce the field sync pulses. Finally, the line and field pulses can be combined to give a composite sync pulse pattern, which should produce interlaced scanning.

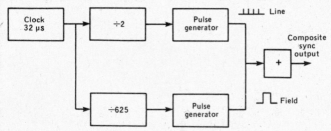

Fig. 41. Block diagram of a simple sync pulse generator

In practice, a more complex sync generator would be used with a much higher primary frequency generator and more complex logic. This would generate half-line field pulses, equalising pulses, and the front-and-back porch signals for blanking to give a full broadcast-standard sync pulse pattern. This involves complex logic, but special integrated circuits have been made which carry out all these functions in one circuit package.

Most home video cameras have a built-in sync pulse generator. This can pose problems if more than one camera is to be used, since each will have its own independent sync timing, making it difficult to mix the two signals. To avoid this, in some cameras the internal sync generator can be run as a slave to an external sync signal. One camera would be used as a master generator, and the others would be locked to it as slaves. In broadcasting studios, this is always done, each piece of equipment being locked to a master sync pattern from the TV network.

How does a colour camera work?

The basic colour-television camera uses three separate vidicon tubes with colour filters in front of each, so that each responds only to red, green, and blue light respectively.

63

Fig. 42 shows the general arrangement of a three-tube colour camera. Colour separation is by means of a set of prisms and dichroic filters. This type of filter uses a very thin layer of metal atoms which permits one colour of light to pass through while reflecting all others. It has the advantage over coloured glass filters that very little light is lost.

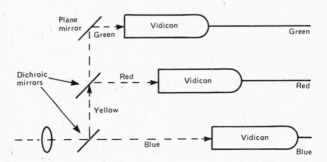

Fig. 42. Optical arrangement of dichroic mirror filters in a three-tube camera

Light from the lens is first passed to a yellow filter, which allows blue light to pass through to the blue camera tube and reflects yellow (red plus green) light. The reflected light passes to a second prism carrying a red filter, which allows green light to pass through to the green tube while reflecting the remaining red light to the red camera tube. The optical paths and positions of the three tubes are set up so that they all view exactly the same image, and all three tubes are scanned simultaneously to produce the R, G, and B components of the colour video signal.

A luminance signal is generated by simply combining the correct proportions of the R, G, and B components to make up the required Y signal. Similarly the R-Y and B-Y colour difference signals can be produced and used in turn to give chrominance signals. Various colour-correction circuits are usually included to give correct colour balance.

Setting up a three-tube camera is quite complicated, as all three images must be accurately registered to avoid any colour fringing effects. This involves not only the optics but also the scanning and synchronisation circuits.

How do single-tube colour cameras work?

For home video cameras the multiple tube arrangement is not really suitable because of its complexity, its size, and the need for accurate registration of the camera tubes. Special camera tubes have been devised for use in home video cameras so that only one tube is required to produce both luminance and chrominance signals. These cameras make use of striped colour filters on the front of the tube and a 'frequency separation' technique to extract the luminance and chrominance signals.

The basic camera tube is normally a vidicon with a 17 mm diameter target. Unlike monochrome tubes, the colour tube has a striped colour filter bonded to its faceplate just in front of the photosensitive target. In a typical tube the colour stripes may be green, cyan and clear, repeated in sequence across the face of the tube. The stripes themselves run vertically down the face of the tube and are very narrow, with typically some 300 sets of stripes across the picture area.

If we consider the light passing through the stripes, all three pass green light. The cyan stripe passes both green and blue (B + G), and the third stripe passes white light (R + G + B). In effect the signal component consists of short variable-amplitude pulses, with one for each set of stripes. The B + G signal consists of pulses twice as wide as those for R + G + B, and again of variable height, while the green signal is continuous. By using a low-pass filter the green component can be separated out. The green + blue component consists of modulated pulses at perhaps 4 MHz and can be extracted using a bandpass filter. The blue signal is obtained by subtracting the green signal. Finally the R + G + B signal is extracted by an 8 MHz filter, then the B + G signal is subtracted to leave the red component. Apart from the R, G and B signals, the luminance (Y) component can also be derived from the multiplexed signal produced by the tube. The four signals (R, G, B and Y) are then encoded into PAL, SECAM or NTSC composite signals as required.

Other arrangements of the colour stripes may also be used. Another typical scheme uses clear (Y), yellow (Y-B) and cyan (Y-R) stripes. Instead of being vertical the yellow and cyan stripes are laid at an angle and have different stripe pitches. The colour separation process again relies on the two colour signals being amplitude-modulated on two different frequencies (related to the stripe pitch); these are passed through frequency filters to separate them and then processed to produce the required luminance and chrominance components.

Because the stripes are very narrow, a camera of this type can usually resolve some 250 to 300 vertical lines across the picture. This is perfectly adequate for home video use, since most videocassette recorders will not reproduce better than 270 lines across the screen. The vertical resolution is of course governed by the TV system (525- or 625-line) being used.

Because of the striped filter the colour tubes are less sensitive than an equivalent monochrome vidicon, but by using wide-aperture lenses typical video cameras have a minimum light sensitivity of around 100 lux. The colour tubes suffer from the same 'lag' problems as other vidicons, and some cameras use a Saticon or Newvicon type of tube with a striped filter to provide better performance under low light conditions.

Sony single-tube colour cameras, such as the HVC2000, HVC3000 and Betamovie, use a special colour pickup tube called a Trinicon. The tube itself is basically a vidicon type with a striped colour filter, but the method used for extracting the colour signals is rather different from the usual frequency-separation technique.

The Trinicon has a colour filter on its faceplate with a sequence of red, green and blue vertical stripes. The important difference in this tube is a clever index electrode, on the face of the photo-sensitive target, which is used to extract the colour information. The index electrode is like a pair of interleaved combs with the teeth precisely aligned with the colour filter stripes. One set of comb teeth overlaps the green and half the adjacent red stripe, while the other set lines up over the blue stripe and the other half of the red stripe. As the beam scans across the tube two modulated signals are produced from the comb electrodes. By reversing the phase of the two signals on alternate scan lines and then combining the signals from one scan line with delayed signals from the previous line, it is possible to separate out the luminance and colour-difference (R-Y, B-Y) signals without using frequency filters. This technique gives improved colour separation and better picture quality than the frequency separation method.

Hitachi colour camera tubes have a striped red, green and blue filter behind the faceplate, but the pickup electrode is also built as a series of thin fingers aligned with the stripes to form three separate interleaved electrodes. The fingers under blue stripes are joined in parallel and brought out to one connection; those under red and green stripes are also paralleled and brought out to two other connections.

The red, green and blue signals are taken directly from the three separate electrodes, amplified and combined to produce the luminance (Y) and chrominance (R-Y and B-Y) signals. The Hitachi technique has the advantage that no complex filtering is required, although the tube is slightly more complex to make, and colour reproduction is very good.

Hitachi use a Saticon-type tube with a target made of selenium, arsenic and tellurium for their more expensive cameras. This type of tube is less affected by lag than standard vidicon types and gives good low-light performance. Some other camera makers, such as Olympus, have also used the Saticon-type tube.

How do solid-state cameras work?

One of the latest developments in video cameras is the charge coupled device (CCD) photosensitive array. This uses an integrated circuit photodetector and makes possible an entirely solid-state camera, which can be very small.

In a CCD camera, the vidicon tube is replaced by an integrated circuit which carries a large array of electronic cells, each of which has a circuit similar to that shown in Fig. 43. The cells are arranged in horizontal rows, one row for each scan line, and each cell in a row deals with one picture element in the line.

Each cell contains a photoconductive resistor R which is coupled through a field effect transistor switch TR1 to a capacitor C1. If TR1 is turned on for a short time, capacitor C1 will charge

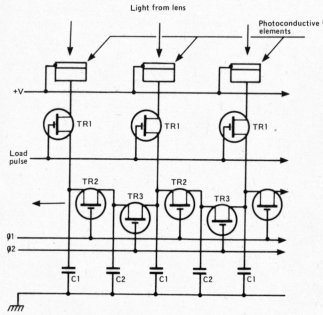

Fig. 43. *Basic circuit of a charge coupled device (CCD)*

to a voltage dependant on the light level falling on the resistor R. If all TR1 switches in a row of cells are switched on simultaneously, a pattern of voltages corresponding to the light pattern for the scan line will be stored in the row of C1 capacitors.

If transistor switch TR2 is turned on for a short time, it will allow the voltage on C1 to be transferred to C2. In the same way, by switching on TR3, the voltage on C2 of one cell can be transferred to C1 of the next cell in the row. If pulses are applied alternately to transistors TR2 and TR3 in the row of cells, the voltage pattern can be shifted along the row from cell to cell and finally out from the last cell in the row. The output signal represents the video signal for the row, and the shifting process is equivalent to the line-scan in a vidicon tube. By taking the output from each row in sequence, a field scan can be achieved and a video output can be generated which represents the image falling on the CCD array.

Using modern integrated-circuit techniques, the cells of the CCD array can be made very small, and a complete sensor can be smaller than the target of a 17 mm vidicon. It is also possible to include within the integrated circuit the video amplifier, sync pulse generator, and scanning logic circuits, so apart from the CCD array, a lens, and a power supply, there is very little in a CCD camera.

There are other solid-state imager devices, such as the charge priming device (CPD) and the MOS (metal oxide semiconductor) type. These also contain an array of photosensitive cells, but the techniques for scanning and signal extraction differ from those of the CCD type.

For colour cameras a striped filter, similar to that used on vidicon tubes, is bonded on to the face of the imager device and the signal separation techniques follow similar lines to those used with vidicon tube cameras.

Solid-state imaging devices do not suffer from 'lag' problems and can have similar sensitivity to that of a vidicon tube. They do, however, suffer from 'blooming', where a very bright area on the screen saturates the cells and activates surrounding cells so that the bright area tends to spread or 'bloom'. Solid-state units are also more robust and have a longer life than vidicon tubes.

What is white balance and how is it set up?

The red, green and blue signals in a camera are set up for true white (no chrominance component) with the camera pointed at a white card. Suppose the camera is set up in sunlight. Under a cloudy sky there is more blue light, so the pictures produced will have a strong blue tint. The light produced by electric lamps contains more red light than daylight, so pictures taken indoors will have a yellowy-orange tint.

In film cameras a coloured filter is placed in front of the lens to correct for differences between daylight and artificial light. A similar technique is used for video cameras. The video camera itself is set up for tungsten lamps where less light is available and maximum camera sensitivity is required. For daylight a yellowy-orange filter is used to give the proper colour balance with some loss in sensitivity. There may also be filters for cloudy sky and tungsten halogen lighting.

As well as filters, a video camera usually has a fine adjustment which allows the sensitivity to be biased towards either red or blue. Often a meter indication is provided which measures chrominance level and the colour balance is adjusted, with the camera pointed at a white card, until a minimum reading is obtained.

6
Videotape recording

What is involved in recording video on tape?

The principles of the videotape recorder are similar to those of the more familiar audio tape recorder, but the recording techniques used are different.

In audio recording, the magnetic tape is drawn over the record/playback head, which is effectively an electromagnet with a very narrow airgap in its magnetic path, as shown in Fig. 44.

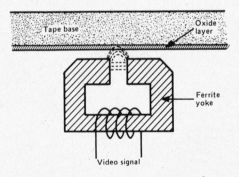

Fig. 44. *Basic operation of tape head*

Audio signals are applied to a winding on the head and produce a varying magnetic field across the airgap. As the tape passes over the head, the field in the airgap causes tiny bar magnets to be

71

formed in the magnetic oxide coating on the tape, producing a varying pattern of magnetism along the tape. During playback, the tape is drawn across a similar (usually the same) head, and the changing magnetic pattern on the tape induces a fluctuating voltage in the head winding. This voltage is then amplified to reproduce the original audio signal.

The major difference between audio and video recording is the bandwidth of the signals involved. In a typical audio recorder, the signal frequencies might range from 50 Hz up to 12 kHz, whereas a video recorder must be able to handle signals ranging from d.c. to 3 MHz or more.

Frequency response at the high-frequency end is governed by particle size on the tape, the width of the head gap, and the speed at which the tape passes over the head. Since the particle size and head gap are limited by physical and mechanical considerations, the tape speed over the head has to be very much higher for video recording than it would be in an audio recorder. Different signal processing techniques and special recording formats are used to handle the wide range of frequencies involved, and the mechanical system needed to handle the tape is usually much more complex.

Is videotape different from audio tape?

Magnetic tape for both audio and video consists of a plastic base (usually acetate, PVC, or Mylar), on which there is a coating of finely divided magnetic powder such as ferric oxide. The coating also contains a binder to keep the oxide particles in place, and a lubricant to reduce friction as the tape passes over the head.

Whereas audio tape is either 3 mm (⅛ in.) or 6.25 mm (¼ in.) wide, a typical videotape for domestic use is 12.5 mm (½ in.) wide, and for broadcast recorders a tape 50 mm (2 in.) wide is used. Tapes for domestic recorders are supplied in cassettes, of which the popular types are VHS, Betamax, and Philips V2000.

Videotape normally has a Mylar base and is made to much higher specifications than audio tape. Particular care is taken to get a smooth oxide surface for minimum head-wear and good contact between tape and head. Videotapes must be kept clean, since dust or fingermarks on the oxide cause bad contact and loss of picture quality. Threading of the tape within a video machine is carried out automatically so that there is no need for the tape to be touched by hand.

What is the extinction frequency?

The extinction frequency is that frequency at which the length of tape occupied by one complete cycle of the recorded signal (i.e., the wavelength) is exactly equal to the effective length of the head gap. At the extinction frequency, the output of the head on replay will fall to zero.

Suppose we have a head with a gap 1μ (one millionth of a metre) long and that the tape is moving past the head at a rate of 1 m per second, then the extinction frequency would be 1 MHz. If a sine wave of 1 MHz had been recorded on the tape, then on replay the situation would be as shown in Fig. 45. The head will respond to changes in the magnetic field across the gap, but in this

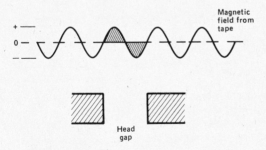

Fig. 45. *At the extinction frequency, the magnetic field in the gap is effectively zero since positive and negative half-cycles cancel one another*

case the positive and negative half-cycles of the recorded field will cancel out, so the head always sees zero magnetic field and will produce zero output. It is assumed that perfect contact exists between the tape surface and the head. In practice, the contact is not perfect, and this has the effect of making the head gap appear to be wider, thus producing a lower value for the extinction frequency.

Videotape recorders normally operate with frequencies below the extinction frequency. At about half the extinction frequency, the signal is roughly 3dB down on its maximum level, and this can be considered to be the effective bandwidth of the recorder. Typical home video recorders have extinction frequencies in the region of 10 MHz, giving a useful signal bandwidth of about 5 MHz. Broadcast recorders are designed to have a much wider bandwidth to give better picture quality.

What is writing speed?

In a magnetic recording system, the writing speed is the rate at which the tape is moving relative to the record or playback head. For any audio recorder or a fixed-head video recorder, the writing speed is in fact the same as the speed at which the tape is moving through the recorder.

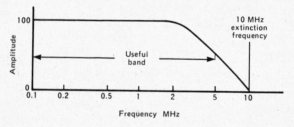

Fig. 46. Response of tape and video head in relation to extinction frequency

On most video recorders, such as broadcast videotape machines and helical scan home videocassette recorders, the head itself is also moving very rapidly, so the writing speed is very much greater than the rate at which the tape travels through the machine. For example, in Betamax home video recorders, the writing speed is 6.6 m per second, whereas the linear tape speed through the machine is only 1.873 cm per second.

What are the basic types of video recorder?

There are three main types of video recorder system. Early video recorders used fixed heads like those of an audio recorder and produced tracks along tape used at very high speed. Recently, machines using a variation of this idea have appeared, such as the BASF and Toshiba LVR systems, but most video machines use rotating-head systems. For broadcast recording, the Ampex Quadruplex system is normally used. Domestic recorders (such as the VHS, V2000, and Betamax systems) use two rotating heads and a helical scanning system.

On these rotating-head systems, sound and a control track for synchronisation during playback are recorded by a pair of fixed heads. These tracks lie along the edges of the tape. In the LVR systems, sound is combined with the video signals and recorded on a single common track.

How does Quadruplex work?

Broadcast videotape machines normally use the Ampex Quadruplex system, in which a 2 in. wide tape runs over a head wheel carrying four heads mounted at 90 deg. intervals around the wheel, as shown in Fig. 47. A vacuum is used to form the tape into a curve across its width so that it makes good contact with the head wheel. As the head wheel rotates, each head writes a transverse track across the width of the tape. All four heads are driven by the same video signal, and since the tape normally wraps around more than 90 deg. of the head wheel, there is an

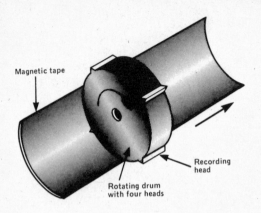

Fig. 47. Layout of a Quadruplex rotating head system, with tape curved to wrap over part of the head drum

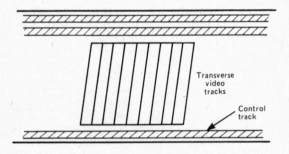

Fig. 48. Track layout on a Quadruplex format video tape

overlap, so one head starts writing its track just before the previous head completes the adjacent track. As the tape moves past the wheel, the successive head tracks are laid side by side, as shown in Fig. 48. Each head writes about 16 scan-lines of the picture across the width of the tape.

The head wheel rotates at either 240 revolutions per second for the American 525-line 60 Hz standard, or 250 r.p.s. for the European 625-line 50 Hz system, and the writing speed is about 40 m per second. The tape itself travels through the machine at a linear speed of either 15 in. per second (USA) or 15.625 in. per second.

A timing signal of 240 Hz or 250 Hz, according to the TV standard in use, is written along a control track at the edge of the tape by a fixed head mounted a short distance from the head wheel. This control signal is used to synchronise the rotation of the head wheel to track position during replay and to control switching of the signals from the heads to give a continuous video output signal. Audio and cue tracks are also recorded along the tape by fixed heads in much the same way.

What is helical scanning and how does it work?

The broadcast standard Quadruplex machines are far too bulky and expensive for domestic use, so a simpler rotating-head system, known as 'helical scan', is normally used in home videotape machines.

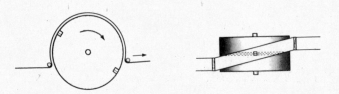

Fig. 49. (a) Path of tape around rotating head drum. *(b)* Side view showing helical path over drum

In the helical scan system, two heads are mounted 180 deg. apart on a rotating drum assembly, as shown in Fig. 49. The tape is wrapped around the drum in a spiral (helical) path, so each head contacts the tape in turn for half a revolution of the drum. As a result, each head traces out a diagonal track across the tape, and as the tape moves slowly past the rotating drum, the tracks are laid side by side along the tape. Spacing between adjacent tracks on the tape is determined by the linear speed of the tape through the machine.

The head drum rotates at 25 revolutions per second for the European 50 Hz system and 30 r.p.s. for the American standard. Thus each revolution of the drum records one complete picture frame and each head writes one field scan on its diagonal track across the tape.

A 25 Hz or 30 Hz timing signal is recorded on an edge track along the tape by a fixed head. This control track is used to synchronise the rotation of the head drum during replay so that the heads read the correct tracks. The audio signal is also recorded on a track along the opposite edge of the tape by another fixed head. A typical layout of the tracks on the tape is shown in Fig. 50.

Since the rotation speed of the head drum is governed by the field-scan rate, the writing speed depends on the diameter of the

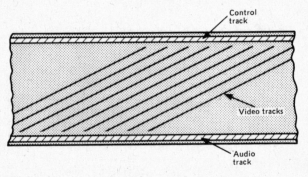

Fig. 50. Typical track layout on helical scan tape

drum. On typical helical scan recorders, a writing speed of 5 m to 8 m per second is normally used. Linear tape speed through the machine determines the spacing from one diagonal track to the next: typical values range from about 1.8 cm per second to 6.5 cm per second.

What is slant azimuth recording?

In early helical scan recorders, problems ocurred with crosstalk, where the head picked up the higher frequency signals from adjacent tracks. To avoid this, the tracks were usually separated by guard bands of blank tape. The disadvantage of this arrangement was that the tape speed tended to be fairly high (around 15 cm per second) and this limited the maximum playing time of a cassette to an hour or one and a half hours.

In an audio recorder, if the head alignment is adjusted so that the gap is at an angle to the recorded track, there is a very rapid falloff in signal at higher frequencies. This property of magnetic recording is used in the slant azimuth system.

In slant azimuth recording, the gap of one of the two rotating heads is set at an angle of 15 deg. to the track path, and the other head is set with its gap at -15 deg. relative to the track. Thus the information on adjacent tracks is recorded at different angles, as shown in Fig. 51. During replay, when the head is reading its own

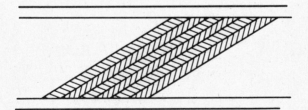

Fig. 51. Layout of track signals with slant azimuth recording

track, the signal output is unaffected, since the head gap is aligned with the recorded information. Signals on adjacent tracks, however, are greatly attenuated, since the head gap is 30 deg. out of alignment with signals from those tracks. By using slant azimuth recording, crosstalk from adjacent tracks is greatly reduced and guard bands are no longer needed between tracks. As a result, the tracks can be packed more closely and the linear tape speed through the machine can be reduced to give much longer playing time for the same length of tape.

How is the luminance signal recorded?

In a video system, the signal with the widest bandwidth is the luminance component, which may cover a range from d.c. up to 3 MHz. In order to handle this wide bandwidth, the luminance signal is recorded on tape by using frequency modulation.

In frequency modulation, the carrier signal has its frequency varied in proportion to the amplitude of the modulating signal. Thus peak white video might give a carrier frequency of 4 MHz, black level might give 3.3 MHz, and the tips of the sync pulses would shift the carrier frequency to 3 MHz. Frequency modulation can easily cope with a d.c. signal, since this will simply be represented by a constant carrier frequency proportional to the d.c. voltage.

The change in carrier frequency produced by a modulating signal is called the 'deviation', and the amount of modulation is often referred to as the 'modulation index' (M), which is given by

$$M = \frac{\text{deviation}}{\text{centre frequency}}$$

where the centre frequency is the carrier frequency with no modulation applied. In video recording, the modulation index is normally less than 0.5.

The frequency-modulated carrier is arranged to have as high a frequency as possible; in a typical recorder, the carrier would swing from about 3.2 MHz for sync tips up to perhaps 4.8 MHz for peak white signal. In theory, an FM signal has infinite bandwidth, but in practical systems frequencies below about 1 MHz and above 5 MHz are filtered off to leave a recorded-frequency band, as shown in Fig. 52.

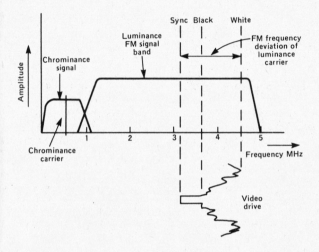

Fig. 52. Bandwidth of signals recorded on video tracks. Note FM deviation and sidebands of luminance and chrominance inserted on low frequency carrier

Frequency modulation is achieved by using the luminance signal to vary the frequency of an oscillator, the output of which is used to drive the recording head. On playback, the signals are amplified and fed to an FM discriminator similar to that used for sound demodulation in a TV receiver. One of the advantages of frequency modulation is that the playback signal is not affected by amplitude changes caused by varying contact between head and tape.

What is meant by 'chrominance-under'?

In broadcast television, the chrominance information is modulated on to a subcarrier frequency (4.43 MHz in Europe) at the high-frequency end of the luminance signal. For tape recording, however, the chrominance is modulated on to a low-frequency subcarrier of about 750 kHz and fitted into the band of frequencies below the FM luminance signal. This is called 'chrominance-under' because the chrominance is tucked in under the luminance signal.

What does a home video cassette recorder contain?

Fig. 53 shows a typical block diagram for the electronics of a video cassette recorder.

To allow off-air recording of television signals, the recorder unit normally contains a receiver section to pick up the required video and sound signals. Most recorders also have direct video and sound inputs to allow a camera and microphone to be used for making programmes.

Luminance signals are fed to a frequency modulator and thence to the recording head. Chrominance is simply shifted in frequency to the required low-frequency subcarrier by mixing it with a fixed oscillator frequency and picking out the difference component from the mixer stage. Audio signals are simply amplified and fed to the fixed head for the audio track. The sync pulses of the television or camera input are recorded as part of the luminance and are also used to correct the speed of the head drum if necessary.

On playback, the luminance is demodulated and the chrominance shifted back to its original subcarrier frequency. Audio is modulated on to a subcarrier, and all three signals are combined to form a composite signal similar to that from a normal television broadcast. This composite signal is used to modulate a VHF or UHF carrier to provide a signal suitable for feeding into the aerial socket of a normal TV receiver.

Many recorders also provide separate video and audio outputs which can be used to drive a television monitor if desired.

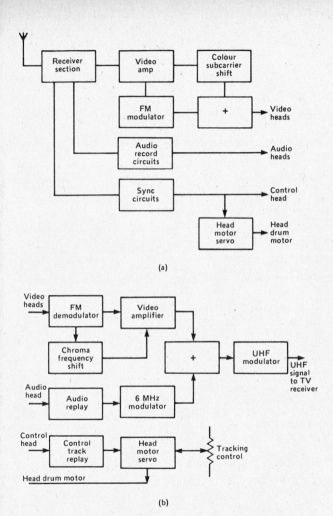

Fig. 53. Video recorder block diagrams. **(a)** Record mode. **(b)** Replay mode

83

The mechanism consists of a rotating-head drum driven by a constant-speed servo system and a second drive system to move the tape through the machine. The tape is contained in a cassette similar to an audio cassette but larger, and there is an automatic threading system to place the tape in its correct path around the

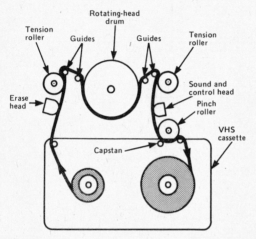

Fig. 54. Tape path in a VHS recorder

drum and the fixed heads. A typical tape path is shown in Fig. 54. An erase head similar to that on an audio recorder is normally fitted.

What are VHS, Betamax, and V2000?

The three currently used systems for home video cassette recorders are the JVC Video Home System (VHS), Sony Betamax, and the joint Philips-Grundig Video 2000 (V2000) system. Of these, VHS is the most popular, closely followed by Betamax.

All three formats use helical scanning with 12.5 mm (½ in) wide tape. Frequency modulation is used for luminance, and the chrominance-under technique is employed. The three cassettes are different in size, Betamax being smallest, and all three have the tape reels side by side. Tapes for one format will not work with machines of the other two formats because of cassette design and the layout of the tracks on the tape.

The VHS system has a writing speed of 4.85 metres/second and a linear tape speed of 2.34 cm/s, giving a typical track width of about 30 micrometres.

These machines use the M-load system shown in Figure 54. Tape is pulled from the cassette and wrapped around the head drum by two solenoid-driven guide pins. The head drum itself is mounted at an angle to the tape path to give the required helical scan, the tape being twisted as it passes over the guide pins. Generally the drum is split into two parts; the one carrying the heads rotates while the other remains fixed. The tape is threaded only when the machine is in a record or play mode, and is unloaded and wound back into the cassette each time the machine is stopped. Some of the latest machines, however, do load the tape for fast forward wind to allow visual picture-search operation.

The Betamax system developed by Sony is basically a scaled-down version of the professional U-matic system, which uses 19 mm ($\frac{3}{4}$ in) tape. In a Betamax recorder the head drum is larger than that for a VHS machine, and the writing speed of 6.6 m/s is the highest for current home video recorders. The linear tape speed is only 1.87 cm/s; this slow speed, combined with a slightly thinner tape, allows the Beta machines to have the smallest cassette for standard home video recorders.

An important feature of the Beta system is the tape path and loading system. The loading system uses a geared rotating ring carrying guide rollers. As it rotates, the ring pulls the tape out of the cassette and gently threads it through the machine as soon as the cassette is inserted. Once loaded, the tape remains threaded around the heads at all times until the cassette is ejected. Because of the relatively easy path and light tape tension this presents no problems with head wear, and in general the handling of the tape itself is much gentler than in the rival systems. The head drum is mounted vertically and the tape is guided round it in a helical path. Most of the drum assembly is stationary and acts as a tape guide. A thin disk, sandwiched between the upper and lower drum sections, carries the heads and rotates.

An advantage of having the tape continuously threaded is that it is an easy task to provide trick effects such as fast picture search and program search on a Beta machine.

Developed by Philips and Grundig to replace the earlier VCR-LP and SVC systems, the V2000 format uses a head drum size intermediate between those of Beta and VHS to give a writing speed of 5 m/s; the tape speed is 2.44 cm/s. The cassette used is about the same size as a VHS type.

A novel feature of the V2000 format is that only half the tape width is used for recording, and at the end of the tape the cassette is turned over to use the other half of the tape width in the same way as for a compact audio cassette. As a result up to eight hours of recording is possible on a single cassette. The tape path is similar to that for a VHS machine but the tape may be left in a threaded condition to permit picture-search operation.

To ensure proper operation with the narrow video tracks, a technique known as 'dynamic track following' is used. In addition to the video signal, a pilot control tone signal is recorded on each diagonal video track. Four different frequencies are used for this control signal, and these are switched in sequence on successive fields of the video recording. The video head picks up the control signals and senses whether the head is running into the adjacent tracks by the relative levels of control signal picked up from the current track and the two adjacent tracks. The head itself is mounted on a small piezoelectric plate; by applying control signals to this head mount, the actual position of the head relative to the video track is continually corrected to keep it at the centre of the track being replayed. This technique theoretically gives perfect tracking and permits very good trick effects such as still frame and picture search.

VHS recorders are produced by JVC, Hitachi, Panasonic, Sharp, Akai and a number of other manufacturers. The Beta system is currently supported by several manufacturers including Sony, Sanyo, NEC and Toshiba. V2000 format machines are produced by Philips, Grundig and one or two other European companies.

How do portable recorders differ from standard machines?

The main requirements of a portable recorder are that it should be compact and not too heavy. This is usually achieved by including only the tape transport and the record/replay electronics in the portable unit and having a separate unit for the tuner/timer and power supply. Power for the portable unit is normally provided by an internal rechargeable battery pack, which also powers the video camera. When the recorder is used at home it is connected to the tuner/timer unit and derives its power from that. The tuner/timer section usually includes a charger for the portable battery pack.

Early portable recorders were relatively bulky and weighed about 6 to 8 kg. By using lighter mechanisms and more complex integrated circuits the weight of modern machines has been reduced to about 3 to 4 kg, which is much more manageable. Betamax portables use a different loading system from the earlier Beta machines to give a more compact transport, but the recordings are completely compatible with other Beta machines. One advantage of Beta machines is that the smaller cassette allows a smaller unit to be produced. To overcome this problem on VHS machines the VHS-C system is used. The VHS-C machines record in the standard VHS format but use a compact cassette giving about 30 minutes running time. The VHS-C tape can be played back on a standard machine by fitting the compact cassette into an adapter which converts it into a standard VHS cassette.

A new 6.25 mm (¼ in) tape format was introduced by Funai and Technicolor for their portable tape system, which was known as the Quarta-Porta or CVC (Compact Video Cassette). This system uses helical scanning with a writing speed of 5.1 m/s and a tape speed of 3.2 cm/s. The cassette is slightly larger than a compact audio cassette and gives about 30 minutes running time. Although this format is not compatible with the 12.5 mm (½ in) machines, tapes can be played back on the CVC machine and transcribed on to a standard VHS or Beta recorder.

Many portable machines, such as the Sony F1 Betamax type, can provide similar facilities to their mains-driven counterparts when combined with a tuner/timer unit. The only disadvantage is that portable systems are generally more expensive than the mains models.

The latest trend in portable equipment is the single-unit camera-recorder (camcorder) such as the Betamovie. This unit is a camera with a miniature recorder system built into it. The recording format and cassette are the same as for standard Betamax, but no playback facility is provided. The recorded cassette may later be played back on a standard Beta machine. Several manufacturers are also developing camera-recorders to use the new 8 mm tape format, which is expected to become a standard for portable use and to replace eventually the Super 8 cine camera.

What is tracking?

When a video recorder is used to play back a pre-recorded tape, or one produced on another machine of the same format, it is possible that the path of the rotating heads may not run along the centre of the helical tracks on the tape. This results in loss of signal and produces a noisy picture or in bad cases picture break-up. The head drum and tape transport servos in the machine are normally controlled by signals picked up from the control track recorded along one edge of the tape. VHS and Betamax machines normally have a 'tracking' control that allows the servo locking to be adjusted until the video head is picking up the best signal from the video tracks. Beta machines seem to be much less susceptible to tracking problems, and although the control is provided it is unlikely to need adjustment.

V2000 machines use control tones recorded along with the video signal to control the actual head position relative to the track as the head drum rotates. Here the actual video heads are mounted on tiny piezoelectric transducers that allow minute changes in head position relative to the drum, and these transducers are controlled by the tone signals. Because of this 'dynamic track following' technique the V2000 machines do not need a control track along the edge of the tape.

What is the running time of video tapes?

For VHS-type machines the standard tape lengths are E60, E120, E180 and E240, giving 60, 120, 180, and 240 minutes running time respectively. The shorter tapes are of the same thickness but different length, whereas the E240 uses a thinner tape to allow it to be packed into a standard VHS cassette. These tapes are for 625-line PAL or SECAM standard machines. For the American NTSC-type machines the standard tape is the T120, which provides 120 minutes running time and is roughly equivalent to the E180 for tape length.

American VHS machines often provide three tape speeds. In standard play (SP) a T120 tape gives 120 minutes, but extended play (EP) and long play (LP) use slower tape speeds to provide 240 and 360 minutes respectively. At the slower speeds picture quality usually suffers somewhat. Some European machines have a long-play mode where the tape runs at half speed to give up to eight hours from a single E240 tape.

Betamax tapes are available in L250, L370, L500, L750 and L830 sizes, where the number indicates the tape length in feet. The most popular sizes are L500 and L750, giving 130 and 195 minutes respectively. The L750 and L830 tapes are progressively thinner than the L500 type.

For V2000 machines the standard tape provides four hours recording on each track to give a total of eight hours. On portable systems the CVC30 (6.25 mm, ¼ in) and the EC30 (VHS-C) tapes each provide about 30 minutes running time. There is also a CVC60 tape giving one hour for the portable machines.

How do trick effects work?

One of the more popular trick effects provided on video recorders is the freeze-frame or still-picture facility. This enables the action to be stopped and a single frame to be continuously displayed on the screen.

To achieve this effect the linear motion of the tape through the machine is stopped, and with the head drum still revolving the video heads trace out the same field tracks continuously.

In practice things are not quite as simple as that. Because the tape is not moving, the path of the video head does not follow the recorded track exactly and tends to move off the track at some point, causing a low signal and possibly crosstalk from the adjacent track. On older machines the effect is to produce a band of noise where the head signal has dropped off. This noise bar may appear at various points on the screen according to where the head is relative to the track when the tape is stopped.

In newer machines careful control of tape position and better signal processing make the noise band much less noticeable and place it near the top or bottom of the screen. Machines such as the Toshiba Beta model and some VHS types use four heads on the drum instead of two. The second set of heads are wider than the normal playback heads and are switched in when freeze-frame is selected. Because these heads overlap adjacent tracks they also stay over the required track throughout the frame, thus removing the drop-out and noise-bar problem. Some machines allow the tape to be run forward or backward one frame at a time.

Visible picture search is obtained by running the tape at higher than normal speed with the head drum still running. This allows a picture to be seen during fast forward or reverse wind operations. The heads move from track to track, picking up bands of picture information with bands of noise as the head moves from one track to the next. Four-head machines reduce or even eliminate the noise bars. The tape may also be run slower than normal to produce a form of slow-motion effect. 'Swing search', provided on some Beta machines, allows normal or slow-speed running both backwards and forwards.

The V2000 system does not suffer from noise-bar problems with freeze-frame and picture search because its 'dynamic track following' scheme keeps the heads aligned with the track at all times.

Some machines provide 'programme search' to help locate a particular programme on tape. Here a marker tone is recorded on the control track at the start of the programme recording. In the search mode the tape is run forward at high speed until the control tone is detected, and the tape is then stopped at the start of the programme segment. If several programmes are recorded on a tape the programme search operation is repeated until the required programme is found.

How do editing and dubbing work?

On early machines, each time the tape was stopped during recording picture break-up and noise bars would be produced on playback as the machine tried to lock on to the signals of the next segment of recording. To provide cleaner editing between one scene and the next, modern recorders use 'roll-back' editing. Here, when the recording is stopped using the pause control, the tape is automatically run back a few frames. When recording starts again the machine locks on to the control and video tracks of the last recorded segment before starting to record the new material. On playback the switch from one shot to the next is then smooth, because there is no disturbance on the control and video tracks.

Audio dubbing allows a new audio track to be recorded over the original without affecting the picture signal. Here the audio erase and record heads are activated alone and the video circuits operate in the playback mode. A separate 'audio dub' button is usually provided to select this mode.

Some machines also provide 'video dub' or 'insert editing' facilities. Here the tape is first run to the end of the section that is to be rerecorded, and the video dub mode is entered with the tape counter set at zero. The tape is then run back to the point where the insert is to start and a new section of audio and video is recorded. When the tape counter reaches zero the machine automatically stops. During video dubbing the video erase head is turned off and a slightly higher level of video signal is applied to the heads to ensure that the old video tracks are fully overwritten. Since the original control track is still on tape, the new material is exactly in synchronism with that already recorded and a clean editing action results.

7
Teletext and viewdata

What is videotex?

The term 'videotex' was coined to describe all information systems, such as teletext and viewdata, by which pages of text and graphic information are broadcast either by radio or through cable networks.

In Britain, all television programmes broadcast by the BBC and ITV carry teletext data as part of the programme signal. Viewdata is represented by the Prestel system operated by British Telecom (formery Post Office Telecommunications), in which data are transmitted through the public telephone network.

An alternative videotex system developed in France is called 'Antiope'. It operates on similar lines to teletext and viewdata but uses different coding for the data signals. A more recent development is the Canadian Telidon system, which can provide high-resolution graphics as well as normal text and graphic pages. In order to give its full potential, Telidon requires a more sophisticated, and more expensive, decoder system.

Various other videotex schemes have been proposed and some have been developed, but it seems that most countries are adopting either the British or French systems, with some modifications to suit local requirements.

What are Ceefax and Oracle?

Ceefax ('see facts') and Oracle (optional reception of announcements by coded line electronics) are the names given to the teletext services provided in Britain by the BBC and ITV networks. Originally, Ceefax and Oracle were two different and rival systems developed in the early 1970s. When a common system for teletext was adopted in 1974, the names were retained to identify the two services.

To use Ceefax and Oracle, a specially adapted TV receiver is required. Having selected the appropriate channel, the viewer uses a calculator-style keyboard to select one of a hundred or more different pages of text being transmitted on that channel. After a short delay, the selected page is displayed on the screen in place of the normal programme picture. At the same time, other viewers can select and display different pages of the teletext magazine.

What is displayed on a teletext page?

A page of teletext information as displayed on the screen consists of 24 lines of text with 40 characters, including blank spaces, in each line.

The text can be displayed in a range of seven different colours: red, blue, green, yellow, magenta, cyan, and white. The background is usually black, but it can be set to any of the text colours, and different combinations of colours can be selected within the same line of text.

Characters can be made to flash on and off, or they can be displayed with twice the normal height to provide emphasis. Some parts of the display can be 'concealed': they will be seen as blank spaces until the viewer operates a button to make the hidden text appear on the screen. This facility is used to conceal the answers to a quiz or puzzle until the viewer wants to see them.

For news flashes and subtitles, a 'boxed' display is used. The normal television picture remains on the screen, but rectangular areas of it are blanked out to form 'boxes' within which the text is displayed.

Apart from the text, a form of graphic display can be used for simple diagrams, graphs, weather maps, and decorative patterns. These can have the same colours as the text.

A typical teletext magazine will have pages carrying news, sports results, travel information, TV programme guides, weather reports, and other general interest items. As with a printed magazine, the layout and the contents are decided by the editor.

Where does teletext data fit into the television signal?

Data signals for teletext are inserted into the blank scan lines that follow the field synchronisation pulses. Four scan-lines in each field are used in Britain: lines 15/18 and 328/331. To allow for future expansion of the service, provision has been made for up to 16 lines in each field to be used for teletext. The arrangement is shown in Fig. 55.

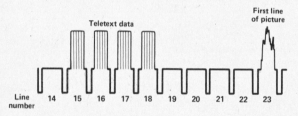

Fig. 55. Locations of the teletext data signals in the field blanking interval

Normally, the teletext data are not visible to ordinary viewers, since the data lines are just off the top of the screen. By reducing picture height or unlocking the field scan, the data signals can be seen as two rows of twinkling dots and dashes just above the top edge of the picture.

What data are contained in a teletext data line?

Each line of teletext represents one row of text in the page that would be displayed on the screen.

94

The data line is divided up into 45 equal segments, called 'bytes'. Each byte represents one character or graphic symbol and consists of a sequence of eight pulses or 'bits'. A bit has a value of either '0' or '1', depending on the signal level. '0' is normally picture black level, and '1' is about 60 per cent of peak white level. Seven of the bits in the byte define the symbol, and the eighth is used as an error check. With seven bits, each of which can be either '0' or '1', there are 128 possible code combinations. Of these, 96 are used for text and graphic symbols, and the other 32 are used for control – to select display colour, to flash symbols, and so on.

In each data line, the first five bytes are used for synchronising the decoder and identifying where the row is to be displayed on the screen. Rows are numbered from 0 to 23, with row 0 at the top of the page. Row 0 is called the 'header' row and, unlike the others, has only 32 text symbols. The first eight bytes after the address code of the row are used to identify the page and to provide various control functions. The format of the header row is usually the same for all pages, giving the name of the service, day, date, and a real-time readout in hours, minutes, and seconds.

Fig. 56 shows the data layout for the header row and the other data rows in the teletext page.

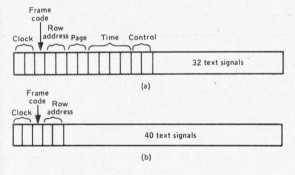

Fig. 56. (a) Data format of a teletext header row. (b) Data format of a normal teletext row

What happens inside a teletext decoder?

Fig. 57 shows a block diagram of a typical teletext decoder system.

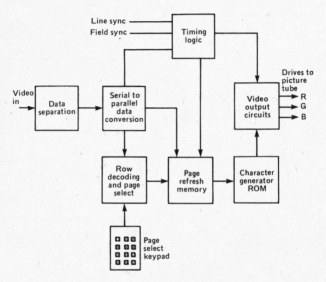

Fig. 57. Block diagram of typical teletext decoder

Video signals from the television receiver are passed to the teletext decoder, where they are processed to extract the teletext data. At this stage, the data signals are cleaned up to remove the effects of noise and distortion introduced by transmission and reception of the signals. The data are also converted from a serial stream of bits to a parallel form, in which all eight bits of each byte are presented simultaneously on eight separate wires, and timing signals are generated to allow each byte in the row of data to be selected and examined.

To select a page, the viewer keys in the required number on a calculator-style keypad, and this number is then stored in the decoder system. As each row of data is received, its row number is checked and all header rows are selected out from the stream. The page number in each header row is then checked against the requested page number, and when a match is found, the following data for that page are written into a page store or memory and will then be displayed on the television screen.

In order to display a page on the screen, the display logic must produce video signals for the complete page every fiftieth of a second and so needs continuous access to the whole page of text data. The received data, however, will be available only once every 30 seconds or so, so a memory system capable of holding a complete page of text is needed to provide continuous access to the text data.

The display logic of the decoder produces the red, green, and blue video drive signals for the display circuits of the television receiver. When the text mode is selected, these signals are used in place of the normal programme picture video to produce the text display on the screen.

How big is a teletext decoder?

The logic involved in decoding teletext is quite complex, and in the early decoders it involved the use of up to 100 integrated-circuit devices. Special large-scale integrated-circuit devices have now been developed for teletext decoders, and a typical modern unit, such as the Texas Instruments XM11 module, will contain perhaps half a dozen integrated circuits on a board measuring perhaps 6 in. (150 mm) by 4 in. (100 mm). Such a module can readily be installed within the cabinet of a television receiver and will normally derive its power from the receiver's supply system.

What is a teletext adapter and why is it used?

Teletext decoder units are normally installed within the TV receiver and wired directly to its internal circuits. This often involves modifications to the normal receiver system, and most units are installed when the receiver was originally built.

Many viewers wishing to use teletext already have standard television receivers and would not wish to modify them. For them, a teletext adaptor unit is the best solution. This is a stand-alone system which is inserted between the receiver and its aerial, and its use requires no modification of the television receiver.

Fig. 58 shows the arrangement of a typical teletext adapter system. The adapter contains its own receiver system to pick up

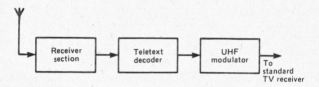

Fig. 58. Block diagram of teletext adaptor

the teletext signals, which are decoded by a teletext decoder module within the unit. The output signals from the decoder are used to modulate a UHF signal to produce a composite vision and sound signal on an unused TV channel. This signal is passed to he aerial input of the television receiver. As far as the television set is concerned, it is merely receiving a TV programme on another channel which just happens to be a text display.

To deal with colour, the adapter unit will usually have a complete colour modulator system. This converts the *R, G,* and *B* outputs of the teletext decoder module into a PAL or NTSC coded chrominance signal, which is then added to the luminance component. Sound from the received programme may be transferred to the output channel.When the text mode is not selected, the unit allows the normal picture signal to pass through. In most adapters, this is done by a UHF link provided between input and output sockets so that, if the TV receiver is tuned to a programme channel, it will be able to pick up the aerial signal directly.

Typical adapter units are the Labgear Colourtext and the Radofin teletext adapter. One disadvantage of the adapter is that the text may not be as sharply defined on the screen display, and colour saturation is usually less than for a direct-drive decoder system.

How are the text symbols generated on the screen?

The text symbols in the displayed page are built up from patterns of dots as shown in Fig. 59. Typically, each symbol uses a matrix

Fig. 59. *Dot matrix layout for teletext symbols to be displayed on TV picture*

which is five dots wide and nine lines high. To separate rows of text and individual symbols in a row, a single line of blank dots is inserted at one side and at the bottom of each symbol space, so the complete pattern for a symbol is six dots wide and 10 lines high.

Patterns of dots for each of the symbols to be displayed are stored in a device called a 'character generator'. This is a memory device similar to those used for the main page memory, but the data patterns are permanently writen into the device when it is made. Such a memory is called a 'read-only memory' or ROM. The dot pattern for a particular symbol is selected from the ROM by applying the data code for that symbol to the inputs of the ROM. By applying a second address code to the ROM, the individual rows of dots for that symbol are set up on the output lines of the device.

To generate the video signal for the display, the system shown in Fig. 60 is normally used. At the start of a scan-line, the code for the first symbol is fed to the ROM, and from its output a pattern of dots for one row of the symbol pattern is transferred into a shift register. The pattern in this shift register is now clocked out

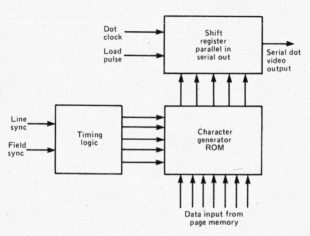

Fig. 60. Block diagram of system for generating dot video for displaying symbols on the screen

as a series of pulses which are on or off according to the dot pattern, and they produce the video signal to generate the dots on the screen. As the scan moves across the line, the codes for the other symbols in the row are fed to the ROM and the corresponding dot patterns are converted to video signals.

On the next scan-line, the next row of dots in the dot matrix for each symbol is called up from the ROM and traced out on the screen. After a complete line of text has been displayed, the patterns for the next line are called up from the page memory, and this process is repeated until the whole page has been built up on the screen.

How are graphic symbols displayed?

Like text symbols, graphic patterns are made up from an array of
dots, but a much coarser matrix is used, only six segments making
up a symbol, as shown in Fig. 61. Because there are not enough

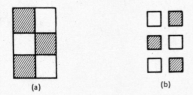

(a)   (b)

Fig. 61. *Two forms of teletext mosaics graphics symbols.* **(a)** *Normal
contiguous graphic symbol.* **(b)** *Separated graphic mode symbol*

data codes to deal with both text and graphics at the same time, a
mode switching scheme is used. When graphic symbols are to be
set into a line of text, a control code is sent which causes the
following symbol codes to be displayed as graphic symbols
instead of text. A second control code is used to switch the display
back to text. These control codes are also used to set the colour of
the symbols being displayed. Control codes are stored in the page
memory just like symbol codes, but they are usually displayed as
blank spaces on the screen.

Most modern decoders use an ROM to produce graphic
patterns in the same way as the text is produced, often with a
single integrated circuit for both text and graphics.

How does viewdata differ from teletext?

The main difference between viewdata and teletext is that
whereas teletext is a one-way system, in which the viewer is
simply selecting one page from a series that is being sent, the
viewdata system provides two-way communicaton between the

user and the central viewdata computer. The user is able to send the desired page number directly to the computer, and only that page of data is sent back for display. This has the advantage of virtually instantaneous response.

A typical viewdata arrangement is shown in the block diagram of Fig. 62. There may by many users connected to the system at the same time, and each has virtually direct access to the computer.

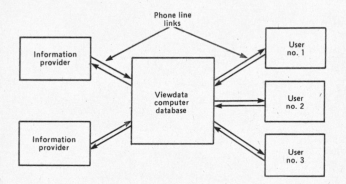

Fig. 62. *Overall arrangement of a viewdata system*

Unlike teletext, viewdata is transmitted along the telephone line character by character, rather than a line at a time. The data coding schemes are virtually the same for both systems. Whereas teletext sends data at about seven million bits per second in very short bursts, the viewdata signals are fed along the line at only 1200 bits per second or 120 characters per second. The transmission from the user to the computer is even slower at only 7.5 characters per second. At each end of the telephone line, a unit called a 'modem' is used to match the signals to the telephone system.

Viewdata decoders are similar to teletext decoders as far as the memory and display are concerned, but the logic for getting data into the memory is different: since viewdata sends only the requested page of text, no page detection is needed.

To use viewdata, the viewer simply dials the telephone number of the viewdata centre. After he has sent a password code, his decoder is linked to the computer and the main index page is sent back along the line and displayed on the screen. The user is now able to select the pages he wishes to see and have them displayed on his screen.

Teletext is normally available free of charge since it is transmitted together with the normal television broadcast. A small charge may be made for some of the pages in a viewdata system, and in addition there will usually be charges for use of the computer and for the telephone call. These charges are usually added to the user's telephone bill.

What is a modem and why is it used?

Public telephone lines are primarily designed for voice transmission and usually have an audio response from about 300 Hz up to 3000 Hz. If digital logic signals are sent along such lines, they are usually distorted, and errors in the received data will occur. To overcome this, a tone modulation scheme is used. In this, a logic '0' level might be represented by a 2100 Hz tone and a '1' by a 1300 Hz tone. The result is a signal as shown in Fig. 63. These audio tones are readily transmitted along the telephone line with little distortion.

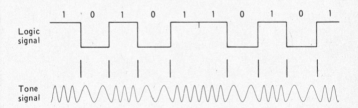

Fig. 63. *Relationship between the viewdata logic symbol and the tone-modulated signal sent over the telephone line*

Data signals are converted into tones by a modulator at one end of the line and converted back to logic signals by a demodulator at the other end of the line. In a two-way system, the modulator and demodulator are combined into a modem at each end of the line. A modem also contains isolation circuits to protect the telephone system from any high-voltage signals produced by the television set.

Sometimes a unit called an 'acoustic modem' may be used. This is not directly connected to the telephone line. It is fitted with a microphone and speaker, and the telephone handset is placed close to these so that the tones are coupled into the phone system as sound signals.

What limits the number of pages in a videotex system?

In teletext, the number of pages on a single TV channel is limited by the access time. This is the time between the user's selecting the page and its appearance on the screen.

If two data lines per field are used for text data and there are 50 fields per second, a page will take roughly a quarter of a second to transmit. For a 100-page magazine, the sequence of pages will repeat every 25 seconds, so this would be the longest time to wait for a particular page to appear in the sequence, and average access time is about 12.5 seconds. With this data rate, the number of pages is limited to 100 to 200 for reasonable access times. If more data lines per field were used, the number of pages could be increased to 800 or 1000.

With viewdata systems, access is virtually instantaneous, since the only delay is while the computer finds the page in its memory banks, which is likely to take less than one second. There is a delay of about eight seconds while the page is transmitted and built up on the screen display. In such a system, the limiting factor is the size of the memory bank available at the computer. The page-address code can have nine digits, allowing direct selection of millions of pages.

How are pages selected on Prestel?

In the Prestel viewdata system operated in Britain, the page-selection system uses a simple tree-type structure. At the start, a main index page is displayed. This gives a set of nine different choices of subject, and the user is invited to key in a number to select one of them. In response to the number, the system sends a further index page with another set of subjects, and again one is chosen. This process can be continued, the information becoming more specific at each step, until the desired subject page is found. Where there are many thousands of pages, this approach enables a user to find a page of information without having to consult a vast index or directory.

The tree allows an alternative way of finding the page required. One of the choices on the main index page is for an alphabetical search. At the second step, the letters of the alphabet are allocated in groups: keying in a '1' might select A, B, and C, a '2' would give D, E, and F, and so on. Using this approach, the subject can be located alphabetically. For pages which are regularly consulted, the user will often know the complete page number and so can key it in directly.

The general idea of the tree address scheme is shown in Fig. 64.

What is telesoftware?

With the rapid increase in the number of home computers, a new service has been added to both teletext and viewdata systems. This is 'telesoftware', by means of which computer programs may be broadcast via teletext or sent along the phone lines to viewdata users.

On teletext a number of pages are set aside for computer programs. On these pages the data no longer represents text for display on the screen but is program data for a computer. By using a suitable adapter unit connected between the TV aerial and the computer and an appropriate program in the computer, the program data can be extracted from the incoming teletext signals and loaded into the computer memory. This works in a similar

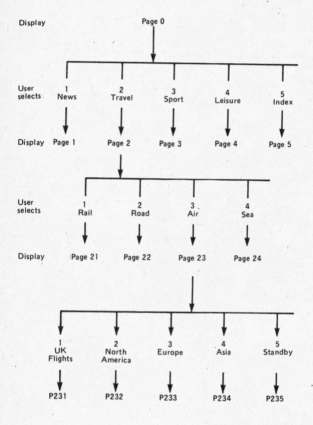

Fig. 64. Tree selection scheme for pages on viewdata

way to loading a program from an audio cassette tape, except that the signals come via teletext. The effective data rate is typically about 300 baud, much the same as for cassette input. Once the program data is in the computer it may be saved on disk or cassette for future use.

At present the BBC broadcasts a selection of programs on CEEFAX which are designed to be loaded into the Acorn-BBC microcomputer. The programs are usually in BASIC language, but there is no reason why other program languages or even machine code could not be used.

Computer programs can also be sent via viewdata. On British Telecom's Prestel service this facility is provided by Micronet 800. For viewdata a modem unit is connected to the computer so that the home computer itself becomes a viewdata terminal. With suitable software the computer calls up the page on viewdata that contains the required program data, and the program is transferred into the computer. This system can work with virtually any home computer capable of being linked to the viewdata system.

What services can be provided by viewdata-type systems?

Because of its two-way nature, viewdata can be used to provide more facilities than the simple information service. Electronic shopping is one application where the viewer is able to call up pages giving lists of goods available and prices. By keying in code numbers and quantities required, one can order the goods from a supplier. Data is automatically sent to the supplier, who then despatches the order. Payment may also be made via viewdata, either by using a credit-card number or by direct funds transfer from the buyer's bank account. This of course requires the bank or credit-card computers to be linked to viewdata, and suitable security safeguards must be provided. Already some building societies and banks are running services on these lines.

Meetings and conferences might be conducted remotely using viewdata, perhaps in association with a television channel. It would also be possible to hold elections using the viewdata system to convey votes to a central computer, which would then calculate the result virtually instantaneously. In France the Teletel viewdata service provides an electronic telephone directory for telephone users in some cities.

An enhanced version of British viewdata allows the inclusion of high-definition colour pictures in the displayed page, and this might be used by advertisers to illustrate their products.

8
TV games and videodiscs

What is a video game?

Most readers will be familiar with the video games that appear in amusement arcades and public houses. These machines all use television screens to provide the game display. The home television games derived from them make use of the domestic television receiver for the display.

A typical TV game unit consists of a control box which governs the conduct of the game, keeps the score, and produces the video signal for the TV display. Remote joystick controllers, connected to the central unit by cables, are provided for the players. The video signals for the display are modulated on to a VHF or UHF signal on an unused TV channel and are fed to the aerial input of the TV set. The display is usually in colour (if a colour set is used), and sound is also provided to give sound effects appropriate to the game being played.

What kind of games can be played?

Early television games units provided four or five 'paddle' games, such as tennis, squash, football, and hockey. The displays were usually simple and crude, with rectangles for the players and a square for the ball. In more recent versions, the court or playing field is shown in perspective, and the players are presented as animated matchstick figures which move around the screen under the control of the players.

The latest units use plug-in cartridges which each provide a different set of games. As an example, the Atari games unit can provide several hundred different games by plugging in a selection of cartridges.

Most of the games fall into one of four basic groups: ball or 'paddle' games, shooting-gallery games, simulations, and strategy games. The ball games vary from simple tennis to baseball and basketball, and in some the motion of the ball is calculated to simulate real conditions. Shooting-gallery games range from simple target practice through cowboy shootouts and aerial dogfights to games such as the popular Space Invaders. In simulations such as Lunar Lander or car racing, the player controls an object on the screen which responds in the same way as it would in real life. In strategy games such as Mastermind and chess, the player pits his wits against the machine. This type of game is invariably controlled by a microprocessor, and often several levels of difficulty are provided. In the most popular games, some elements of all four types of game are included to provide maximum interest.

What is inside the game control unit?

Fig. 65 is a block diagram showing the typical works of a television-game unit. Signals from the players' controls are fed to the control logic section, which governs the action of the game and the scoring. Signals from this section then pass to the display-generation logic to control the display. In the display logic, a composite line and field synch pulse-pattern is generated, and to this is added a luminance video signal representing the desired display on the screen. For colour, the appropriate R, G, and B chroma signals are produced, and an audio signal is generated for sound effects. Chroma signals are then encoded on to a subcarrier in either the PAL or NTSC coding, and the audio is also used to frequency-modulate a second sound subcarrier. Finally, the luminance, chrominance, and sound signals are combined and modulated on to a VHF or UHF signal to produce an output suitable for feeding to the aerial input of a standard TV receiver.

110

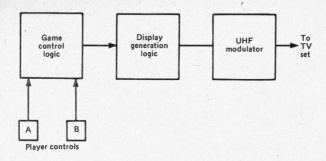

Fig. 65. Block diagram of basic TV game

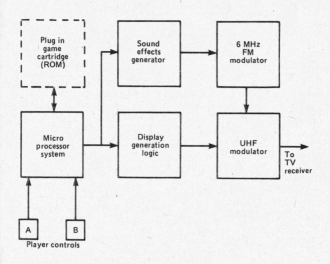

Fig. 66. Block diagram of microprocessor plug-in cartridge game system

111

Although most early games units used special integrated circuits for the control and display logic, most modern units employ a microprocessor system, although the generation of the video and sound signals may use a separate integrated circuit.

What is inside a game cartridge?

Although early games had a special game control circuit in the cartridge, microprocessor systems normally use a read-only memory (ROM) device in the cartridge. This ROM has the computer program for the set of games permanently written into it. When a game is selected by a control on the games unit, the microprocessor reads the appropriate section of the program from the ROM and executes it to control the game.

How is the game display produced?

In the early types of TV game, the players, balls, and other objects on the screen were generated by analogue methods, using a scheme like that shown in Fig. 67.

A variable delay triggered by the line synch pulse is in turn used to trigger a short-pulse generator to produce a pulse whose position across the line-scan can be varied. A similar delay and pulse-generator circuit is driven from the field synch pulse. The outputs of the two pulse generators are then gated together so that an output pulse occurs only when both delayed pulses are present. If this gated pulse is now used as a luminance signal, a bright rectangle will be produced, and the screen and its position can be varied by varying the lengths of the two delays. Similar circuits are used for each of the moving objects. Fixed objects like the net or boundary are produced using fixed delay circuits.

For microprocessor systems, the display video is generated in much the same way as for a teletext system. The various objects (players, spaceships, cars, and so on) are treated as symbols and made up from a pattern of dots in a character generator ROM. To place an object at a particular point on the screen, the

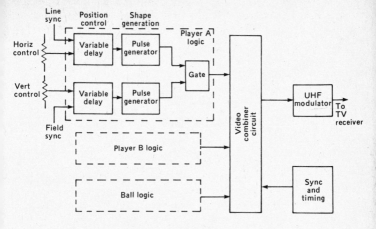

Fig. 67. *Position control and player symbol generation logic for a simple TV game*

processor simply writes the symbol code for the object into the appropriate location in the display memory, and the display circuits will generate the required pattern of dots at that point on the screen. When a player symbol is animated, a sequence of different patterns is called by the processor as the symbol moves on the screen, and the arms, legs, or body patterns are changed to simulate the desired motion.

How do the players' controls work?

The players' controls are usually potentiometers mounted on a joystick. One of the potentiometers responds to sideways motion of the joystick, while the other responds to forward and backward movement. Diagonal motion produces proportional changes in both of the potentiometers. A pushbutton switch is usually provided for events such as firing a missile, and in some controls a third potentiometer is used to sense twisting motion of the joystick.

In simple games, the potentiometers control the delay circuits which position the player or other object on the screen. Microprocessor systems usually convert the potentiometer signals into numbers representing the position of the object.

How is a hit or score detected?

In any shooting type of game, hits are detected by comparing the position of the two objects concerned. In the early games, this was done by simply gating the pulse pattern representing one object with that of the other. If at any time the pulses occur simultaneously, then some part of the two objects must be in the same place and therefore a hit has been made.

In microprocessor systems, a similar principle is used, but the position and size of each object is given by a set of numbers in the computer's memory, and these are compared to see if they coincide in order to detect a hit. Often this is done by simply comparing the symbol locations in the display memory to see if the objects are in the same position.

Can a TV game damage the picture tube?

Some controversy has arisen over this. In the arcade game, where direct video drive to the display is used and the game is running continuously for many hours, it is possible that after some time a permanent image of the static parts of the display may be produced on the screen by continuous bombardment of the phosphor.

With a home video game, assuming that the brightness and contrast are set up for a normal TV picture, it is unlikely that such an effect could occur: the display would have to be excessively bright for very long periods to produce any harmful effects. In many modern games, the display changes from time to time even in the same game, so that continuous use of the same areas of the screen is avoided. This reduces still further the chances of damaging the TV tube.

What is a video disc?

A video disc is the equivalent of the audio LP record. Like an audio record, it consists of a plastic disc some 30 cm (12 in) or 20 cm (8 in) in diameter, on each side of which is a spiral track or grooves which carries the video signal information. When inserted into a suitable player, the disc rotates, and a pickup device, following the spiral track, detects the information to produce video signals. These video signals and the accompanying audio are amplified and used to modulate a VHF or UHF signal which is fed to the aerial terminals of a TV receiver in order to display the programme recorded on the disc.

   Programmes on video discs are pre-recorded, and the discs are pressed from a master in much the same way as for audio discs. Compared with videotape, a video disc is cheap to manufacture and therefore should sell at a lower price than a pre-recorded video cassette.

Are there different types of video disc?

As with videotapes, there are several different forms of video disc. Two major techniques are used to put video informaton on disc. One uses capacitance variations between the disc tracks and a pickup stylus to carry the video information; the other makes use of an optical system. Capacitance discs are represented by the RCA Capacitance Electronic Disc (CED) and by the JVC VHD disc system. The optical technique, involving a laser, is used by Philips.

How does an optical disc work?

The disc for an optical player is made from a reflective material. Video signals are stored as a pattern of tiny shallow pits along the spiral track on the surface. Unlike an audio disc, this type of video disc has no groove for the track. A small helium-neon laser is used to produce a very sharply focussed spot of light which is made to follow the spiral path of the signal track. The pits in the track cause variations in the reflected light from the surface of the disc, and these are picked up by a photocell and amplified to produce a signal from which the recorded video and audio information can be derived. As with videotape, the video signal recorded on the disc is frequency-modulated.

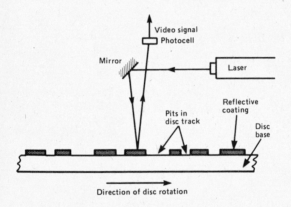

Fig. 68. *Principle of the Philips LaserVision disc, showing a section through one of the tracks*

There are two types of optical disc, known as CAV (constant angular velocity) and CLV (constant linear velocity). In the CAV type, the disc rotates at 1500 rev/min (1800 rev/min for American players), so each rotation represents one complete picture frame. This type of disc provides 30 minutes of programme on each side of the disc.

Optical players are usually designed to handle both CAV and CLV discs. The playback mode may be selected automatically by sensing coded information on the disc when it is inserted in the player.

In Europe, the optical disc is represented by Philips' Laser-Vision; in the USA, players are produced by Pioneer (Laserdisc) and by Magnavox (Magnavision). Discs produced for American players are not compatible with European players because of the different television standards involved.

How do capacitance discs work?

In the RCA CED system, the disc has a shallow spiral groove for the video track much like the groove of an audio disc. Along the bottom of the groove is a pattern of shallow pits similar to those on an optical disc. The disc is made from, or coated with, a conductive material. A diamond stylus carrying a metal electrode

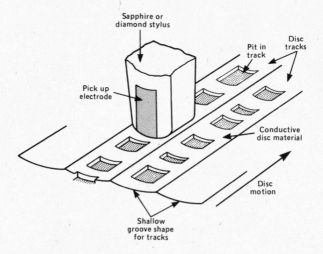

Fig. 69. General arrangement of tracks and pickup on an RCA disc

follows the groove, and variation in capacitance between the electrode and the disc, produced by the pits, is detected and used to produce the video and audio signals.

RCA discs, marketed under the name 'Selectavision', normally run at 450 rev/min for the American system, giving four complete

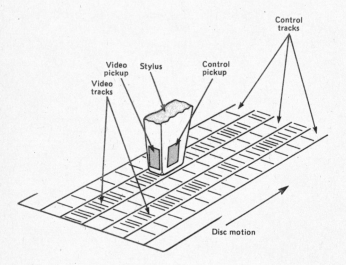

Fig. 70. Layout of video and control tracks on a JVC VHD disc

frames per revolution. A disc provides one hour of programme from each side.

The JVC VHD system also uses a conductive disc, but it has no grooves. An extra control track is placed alongside the video track and is used to provide a guidance signal for the stylus which runs on the surface of the disc. The stylus carries electrodes additional to the one used to sense the programme signal. These extra electrodes pick up signals from the control tracks on each side of the video track and produce control signals for the stylus-arm servo system to keep the stylus in the centre of the video track. The main advantage of this scheme is that stylus wear is greatly reduced.

Discs for the JVC VHD system run at 900 rev/min for the American standard and 1000 rev/min for the European standard. Each disc provides one hour of programme on each side.

How do the disc systems compare?

As far as picture quality goes, all three systems seem to produce good-quality pictures, although the laser system is capable of a wider video bandwidth and may be less noisy. Certainly, the laser system produces no wear on the discs, since there is no physical contact. Of the two capacitance systems, the JVC VHD gives reduced stylus wear and so longer stylus life. The capacitance systems have the advantage of being simpler and probably cheaper to manufacture, since they do not require a laser and an optical system.

One advantage of the CAV optical system is that it is easy to provide a still-frame facility, since one frame is recorded per revolution.

Index